WICCA
LOVE
SPELLS

Also by Gerina Dunwich

Candlelight Spells
The Concise Lexicon of the Occult
Wicca Candle Magick
Wicca Craft
Circle of Shadows (poetry)

WICCA
LOVE
SPELLS

GERINA DUNWICH

CITADEL PRESS
Kensington Publishing Corp.
www.kensingtonbooks.com

CITADEL PRESS BOOKS are published by

Kensington Publishing Corp.
119 West 40th Street
New York, NY 10018

Previously published as *The Secrets of Love Magick*.

All Kensington titles, imprints, and distributed lines are available at special quantity discounts for bulk purchases for sales promotions, premiums, fund-raising, educational, or institutional use.

Special book excerpts or customized printings can also be created to fit specific needs. For details, write or phone the office of the Kensington sales manager: Kensington Publishing Corp., 119 West 40th Street, New York, NY 10018, attn: Sales Department; phone 1-800-221-2647.

CITADEL PRESS and the Citadel logo are Reg. U.S. Pat. & TM Off.

ISBN-13: 978-0-8065-4129-7
ISBN-10: 0-8065-4129-6

First Citadel trade paperback printing: January 1996

10 9 8 7 6 5 4 3 2

Printed in the United States of America

Electronic edition:

ISBN-13: 978-0-8065-3980-5 (e-book)
ISBN-10: 0-8065-3980-1 (e-book)

I dedicate this book with loving gratitude to the following beautiful people: Al B. Jackter, my Gemini lover, friend, and inspiration; my mother, Teri LoMastro, who has more love in her heart than anyone I know; Barbara Jacobson, for her love, laughter, and friendship; and, of course, my publisher for making this book possible.

Contents

WICCA
LOVE
SPELLS

Introduction:
All You Need Is Love

Love magick, ancient in origin, has been practiced for countless centuries on every continent by every culture in one form or another.

Love potions and love spells are two of the most popular and best-known examples of love magick, but there are many other elements as well, including charms, amulets, talismans, herbs, omens, astrology, palmistry, and the divinatory arts, just to name a few.

In the United States, love magick is a common practice among the Creoles, Hoodoos, the Voodoo Queens of Louisiana, and the Native American Indians. It is also practiced by most modern Witches in every state of the country.

Among nearly every North American Indian tribe, various forms of love magick have been practiced, notably by the Canadian Indians known as the Cree. Their reputation as "love magicians" is greatly respected (and often feared) by many of the surrounding Indian tribes.

In Great Britain, love magick was the most popular type of magick, and some form of it was practiced by nearly all Witches, especially on Saint Agnes' Eve (see Glossary of Terms) and Saint Valentine's Day.

Saint Valentine's Day, observed to acknowledge love and romance, is (like most of our modern holidays) Pagan in origin and stems from the Lupercalia, an ancient Roman fertility festival celebrated on the fifteenth day of February in honor of Lupercus, a fertility god similar to Pan and Faunus. It is said to have been established by Romulus and Remus, although other evidence suggests that it is probably older than Rome itself.

During the festival, young men chose their sexual partners by drawing the names of young women out of a bowl. (This is most likely the origin of our modern valentine custom.)

As the influence of the Christian church began to take over the Old Religion, the Pagan fertility god was replaced by their Saint Valentine. February 14 was named Saint Valentine's Day, following the tradition in supplanting the old Pagan holidays.

In Europe, many plants (in particular the mandrake) have been widely used in love magick. Aphrodisiacs and love philtres made from ginseng and other exotic plants are common in the Orient, and various animal parts are popular love-potion ingredients in Africa, Haiti, Cuba, and Australia.

Love magick is simple and easy to use. Its popularity is increasing, and nearly everybody has practiced it at one time or another (either consciously or unknowingly), even if only by one of the most simple forms, say, breaking a wishbone and wishing for a lover, wearing jewelry (love charms) to make oneself attractive, or reading a horoscope column to gain information or advice about one's love life.

In the sixteenth and seventeenth centuries, to "provoke another to unlawful love by means of magick or witchery" violated the law. It was punishable by imprisonment, torture, and sometimes even death.

Luckily, today the ridiculous laws against witchcraft and magick are no longer a threat to anyone; however, in certain places witchcraft remains misunderstood and socially unaccepted, and one has no choice but to be forced into secrecy to protect his or her craft or else run the risk of being subjected to public ridicule, discrimination, job loss, and possibly even violence.

We sincerely hope all of this will change someday and that men and women of all religious beliefs, as well as all customs, races, colors, creeds, and sexual orientations, will be able to accept each other and live together on the same planet in peace, harmony, and love.

"DO WHAT THOU WILT SHALL BE
THE WHOLE OF THE LAW.
LOVE IS THE LAW, LOVE UNDER WILL."

1

The Secrets of Love Magick

Love magick can be used to send out your own personal love vibrations to attract the right lover or spouse, make yourself more desirable and "magnetic" to the opposite sex, and set the proper magickally charged atmosphere in which love can bloom.

Once the spark of love is magickally ignited, however, the fate of the relationship is entirely up to you and your love partner. Magick can bring two people together, but it cannot force another person to love you or stay married to you against his or her will. Magick cannot join two people together for life if they are not karmically correct for each other. (Any person who tells you otherwise is either a liar, a fraud, or an unenlightened person who doesn't know the first thing about how true magick works.)

Love magick can be performed by both men and women (gay, Lesbian, or straight) to attract a lover, a soulmate, or even the platonic love of a friend or a relative.

Before performing any love spell, be absolutely sure that you are sincere and emotionally prepared to enter into a new love relationship with another person. However, if you are only interested in attracting a lover into your life for sexual pleasure rather than for a lasting, meaningful love relationship, it is best for you to work with aphrodisiacs and passion spells, and not use love magick.

Most love spells should be performed on a Friday and only during the waxing phase of the moon—the time ranging from the new moon through the first quarter to the full moon. Consult an up-to-date astrological or lunar calendar.

Magick to end a love affair or reverse a love spell should be performed when the moon is in a waning phase—the time ranging from the full moon through the last quarter to the new moon.

One of the most important elements in the practice of love magick is feeling. It is absolutely essential that you possess strong feelings about what you are attempting to accomplish in order to produce the power needed to perform magick. For instance, if you are working a love spell to help a friend and her estranged husband get back together, you must strongly feel in your heart that it is right for these two people to be back together. You must sincerely want them to make up with each other and be reunited. The same thing applies whenever you are working love magick for yourself.

It is also very important to use creative visualization (also known as "willed imagination"). This is the magickal art or skill of imagining the end results of your magick in order to make your desires materialize. It is a natural, Goddess-given ability in certain people, but most of us need to activate and cultivate our powers through much practice, concentration exercises, and meditation.

When spellcasting, always concentrate deeply and get a clear mental picture of what (or who) you want or need. For example, while you are casting a love spell or crafting a special amulet to return a lost lover, see in your mind the image of your lover and yourself happily back together.

Without feeling and creative visualization, it is extremely difficult, if not absolutely impossible, for love magick to work.

You will find that better results are achieved if you work love spells yourself and/or make your own amulets and philtres rather than have someone else (especially a stranger) perform the magick for you. When you perform a spell for yourself, you empower the magick with your own emotional and spiritual vibrations.

Use love magick wisely, cautiously, and only in a positive way. All magick is serious business and should never be abused or treated as a game or as a joke. Always keep in mind the Wiccan Rede of Witches which states: "AN IT HARM NONE, DO WHAT THOU WILT." Do your own thing, just as long as you don't harm anybody. If you do bad unto others, the bad will return to you threefold. This same karmic law of retribution applies whenever you do something positive—three times the good will come back to you.

Never attempt to use love magick to manipulate another person's will or emotions. Apart from the fact that no amount of love magick can ever enslave another person to you or turn your beloved into a mindless, emotionless love-slave, magickal manipulation falls into the category of black magick, and can bring disastrous results. Use love magick to attract love or to spark a romantic interest, not to manipulate or enslave another human being.

To avoid being manipulative, many Witches suggest you should perform spells to attract a lover in general and not a particular man or woman. If you desperately desire the affections of another, however, you can cast a perfectly "legitimate" love spell by sincerely adding to it (or your request to the gods) an expressed desire to attract and hold fast that person's love, but only if you are karmically right for each other and no harm will come of it. If you perform such a spell insincerely, be warned that it could easily backfire!

Before performing love magick, it is always wise to do a divination of some kind to find out whether the results of your magick will be positive or negative. For example, if you desire the love of a certain man who is currently in love with someone else, and you selfishly cast a love spell on him, the spell may have serious consequences. You might win his love, but only at the expense of his lover's accidental death. In such an event, your love magick (even though unintentional) would have the same effect as evil black magick. You would be subject to threefold bad karma and probably end up losing his love anyway. Always do a divination first, just to be on the safe side, and consider all possible consequences before you act.

For a divination, you may use a crystal ball, Tarot cards, candles, rune stones, or whatever method you prefer. If you are not yet skilled in the art of divination, consult an experienced Witch or a reputable master of the occult arts. Beware, however, of so-called "professional sorcerers" or mystical New Age gurus who promise miracles and charge outrageous fees to perform them. Unfortunately, many of these people are nothing more than frauds and charlatans who are out to make a fast buck at your expense. (Most Witches who are for real do not advertise their Craft in public. The few who do make a living by it usually accept donations for their services in lieu of charging a specific fee). As with anything else, be cautious, check around, and use common sense. If something sounds too good to be true, it probably is!

Love magick is powerful and it works; but certain spells may have to be repeated several times to get them right, especially if you are a beginner or a novice Witch. (If you are new to magick, don't be discouraged by early failures. With proper training and practice, you will soon get a "feel" for magick and be able to use its powers to work for you.)

To sum it all up, to perform successful love magick, one must be in harmony with the laws of nature and the psyche. It is important to possess magickal knowledge, a healthy body and mind, and the ability to accept responsibility for one's own actions. It is impossible to obtain positive results magickally if you have a low energy level, or contaminate your system with harmful drugs and/or excessive amounts of alcohol. Working during the proper lunar phase, having the conviction, concentration, and visualization of the end result—these are the principal secrets of successful love magick!

Feel free to change and adapt any love spell described in this book to suit your personality and special needs. Remember—all spells are only as powerful as the energy one puts into them.

2

Spellcraft

To Reverse Any Love Spell

On a night when the Moon is in a waning phase, write your name and the name of your bewitched lover on the side of a white votive candle. Anoint the candle with myrrh oil, light it, and say:

I BURN THIS CANDLE AS A TOKEN

OF THE SPELL THAT BINDS OUR LOVE.
LET THIS MAGICK NOW BE BROKEN
BY THE POWER OF THE GODS ABOVE.

Allow the candle to burn itself out. After the leftover wax has cooled and hardened, wrap it in a piece of white silk, tie it tightly with a white ribbon, and then toss it into the sea or into a river.

Blood Spell

To win the affections of a certain man or woman, put a drop of his or her blood on a cone of patchouli or rose-scented incense, and say:

BLOOD OF (name of your beloved)
LOVE OF (name of your beloved)

Put a drop of your own blood on the incense cone and say:

BLOOD OF (your name)
LOVE OF (your name)

Light the incense and pass a red apple three times through the smoke. With a consecrated athame, slice the apple in half. Eat one half and then give the other to your beloved to eat. (The spell should begin to take effect immediately after he or she eats the apple.)

Venus Pentacle Spell

To improve your love life, perform this spell on a Friday
when the moon is in the sign of Taurus: Take a Venus Pentacle (available at most occult shops and through mail
order catalogues) and place it in the middle of an altar between two pink or red candles. Light the candles and then
anoint the Pentacle with a drop of musk oil. Say:

> PENTACLE OF VENUS
> GODDESS OF LOVE AND DESIRE
> I CONSECRATE THEE AS A TOOL OF LOVE
>   MAGICK
> AND IN THE SACRED NAME OF THE GODDESS
> I CHARGE THEE NOW WITH LOVE-DRAWING
>   POWER.
> SO MOTE IT BE!

Carry the consecrated Venus Pentacle in your pocket,
purse, or charm bag as a powerful love-drawing amulet, or
sleep with it under your pillow on Saint Agnes' Eve to see
the face of your future lover in a dream.

To Make the Person You Love Desire Marriage

Gather an Adam and Eve root on Saint John's Eve and powder it by the light of a red candle. Mix the powder with a bit of sand and a few drops of blood from the ring finger of your left hand. Write your name in the sand mixture and then, when the time is right, sprinkle a bit of it in the hair of the intended spouse.

A Modern Witch's Love Philtre

Required are passion flowers, patchouli leaves, basil, cloves, and sweet red wine. The herbs are powdered and mixed together by the light of a red (or pink) candle and put into the wine which is then given to the intended lover to drink.

When preparing philtres or casting love spells, it is important to concentrate always on the man or woman whose affections you desire. Chant his or her name over and over as you work the love magick, visualizing yourself and that person as passionate lovers. Creative visualization truly is the key to successful magick!

To Attract a Lover

According to Newfoundland Witches, you must take a red apple and prick it full of holes with a needle as you recite aloud the name of your beloved. On a night of the new moon, sleep with the apple under your pillow. The following morning, wash and core the apple, mash it, and add it to the filling of a homemade apple pie, which is then given to your intended lovemate to draw him into love. (The mashed apple may also be used in numerous cookie or cake recipes.)

To Gain a Prophetic Dream of One's Future Love

Recite the following magickal incantation as you pluck a sprig of the mystical ash tree:

ASHEN-TREE, ASHEN-TREE
I PLUCK THEE.
THIS NIGHT MY TRUE LOVE
FOR TO SEE.

Place the sprig under your pillow when the moon is full, and your future lover or spouse will appear before you in a dream.

Three Modern Witch's Spells to Return a Lover

Spell No. 1: Prick the ring finger of your left hand with a pin of silver, and with some of the blood, write both your name and the name of your parted lover on a circle-shaped piece of white silk. With ashes of burnt basil (the sacred herb of Love), draw one circle around both names on the silk as you visualize your lover returning to you. Fold the piece of silk in half, and then fold it over one more time. Stick the silver pin through the folded silk to hold it together, and then bury it deep in the soil of Mother Earth at midnight on the third night of the waxing moon.

Spell No. 2: On a night of the new moon, nail a branch of myrtle (sacred to Venus) over the front door of your house and allow it to remain there throughout the waxing phase of the moon to magickally draw your lover back to you.

Spell No. 3: For effectiveness, the following magical love spell should be performed on a Friday night when the waxing moon is either in the sign of Taurus or Libra. (Venus, the planet of love and desire, is the ruler over these two astrological signs of the zodiac. It is also the ruling planet of the sixth day of the week.) Stick a needle through the wick of a dark red candle if your lover is a man; or a pink candle if your lover is a woman. Light the candle and visualize your lover returning to you as you recite this magickal incantation:

LIGHT OF VENUS LIGHT OF LOVE
BURN IN (name) HEART
AND RETURN HIS/HER LOVE TO ME.
SO MOTE IT BE.

The Circle of Light Love Spell

On a night when the moon is in a waxing phase, anoint twelve white candles with rose oil and arrange them to form a circle around you, starting in the East. In the center of the circle, place an incense burner filled with African violet incense and a photograph of the man or woman whom you desire love from. Sit or kneel before the photograph, light the incense and candles, and say:

AS THIS CIRCLE OF LIGHT SURROUNDS
    HIS (HER) IMAGE
SO SHALL MY LOVE SURROUND HIS
    (HER) HEART.
AS THIS FRAGRANT INCENSE BURNS
    WITH FIRE
HIS (HER) BURNING DESIRE FOR ME
    SHALL START.
HIS (HER) LOVE FOR ME GROWS
    STRONGER
AS THESE TWELVE CANDLES BURN.
AS LOVE IS GIVEN, SO SHALL IT
    RETURN.
SO MOTE IT BE.

Gaze into the photograph and visualize a red, glowing beam of love- energy emanating from your body into the picture. As you concentrate and visualize, chant out loud the name of your beloved.

After the candles have burned down, give the wick ends to the one you desire to help him (or her) fall passionately in love with you.

The Broken Mirror Spell

To bind a lover to you, smash to pieces a small mirror into which the man or woman from whom you desire love has gazed. Take the broken pieces of glass and bury them in a flowerpot filled with dirt during the waxing phase of the moon. Place the flowerpot on a windowsill facing West, and sprinkle it every Friday with a tea made from spikenard and rainwater as you chant aloud your desired lover's name.

To Ease the Agony of Unrequited Love

Light a fire in the fireplace on a night when the moon is in
a waning phase and cast a handful of dried vervain into
the dancing flames.

To Bring Back an Unfaithful Lover

Gather the root of elfwart (elecampane) on Saint John's Eve. Powder the root and mix it with the grated rind of an orange and some ambergris. By the light of a red candle, write your lover's name on a piece of paper, using red ink, and burn it. Stir the ashes into the powdered root mixture as you thrice recite his (or her) name, and then place it in a small box, along with a lock of his hair, a thread from his clothing, and two figures (one male and one female) fashioned from the stalks of hay. Tie seven red strings with seven tight knots around the box. Place it in a dark, undisturbed spot for seven nights, and then anonymously mail it to the unfaithful lover to cause him (or her) to return to you within seven days.

To Make a Man Want to Marry You

According to one of the most powerful and best-known spells of the Santeria Witches, you must hollow out the root of a lily and fill it with lamp oil. Over the oil, place a floating wick made of a cotton wad soaked in the man's semen (the symbol of his manhood). Light the "oil lamp" at 9:00 P.M. every evening for one hour, and the man will soon submit himself to the will of the Witch who burns the lamp.

Cuban Love Spell

Write your beloved's name on a yellow nine-day candle
five times with your own name written across it five times.
Dress the candle with a mixture of rose oil and powdered
maidenhair fern. Place the candle inside a glass container,
and say:

BLESSED BE WITH POWDERED FERNS
BLESSED BE WITH OIL OF ROSE
AS THE CANDLE FIRE BURNS
SO THE LOVE VIBRATION GROWS.

Place a photograph of your lover in a small dish. Cover
it with a bit of honey and arrange five small fishhooks over
the photo. Dip your finger into the honey and taste it. (The
love-goddess Oshun will not accept any offerings unless
they are tasted in her presence.) Light the candle in the
name of the Goddess, and say:

BY THE POWER OF THE GREAT OSHUN
GODDESS OF LOVE, PASSION, AND BEAUTY
I CAST THIS SPELL OF LOVE UPON (name).
LET HIS LOVE AND PASSION
BURN ONLY FOR ME
UNTIL I SET HIM FREE FROM THIS SPELL.
SO MOTE IT BE.

Cuban Spell To Return a Reluctant Lover

Hollow out a pumpkin and put five toenails from a rooster inside it along with an egg, pepper, marjoram, Florida Water, a small personal article from your lover (such as a lock of hair, a piece of thread from his clothing, jewelry, etc.), and his name written on a piece of paper. Spit inside the pumpkin three times and then place it in front of an image of the love- goddess Oshun for ten days. After the time has passed, throw the pumpkin into a river and your lover will soon return to you.

Medieval European Marriage Spell

Find nine peas and place the pod on the lintel of your kitchen door to attract a husband to your house.

Witch Candle Spell

On a Friday evening, place a pink or red Witch-shaped candle on a 24" × 24" piece of aluminum foil, folded in half. Write the name of the man or woman from whom you desire love on the bottom of the Witch candle and then anoint it with some rose, musk or patchouli oil. Light the candle and recite the following incantation three times:

> WITCH CANDLE
> WITCH CANDLE
> BRIGHT WITH FIRE,
> INFLUENCE THE SPIRITS
> TO BRING ME MY DESIRE.

Allow the candle to burn down one inch each day. After it has burned all the way to the bottom, wrap the aluminum foil tightly around it and place it under your bed.

After seven days and nights, throw the foil-covered Witch candle into a river, and say:

> WITCH CANDLE
> WITCH CANDLE
> LET YOUR MAGICK BIND.
> WITCH CANDLE
> WITCH CANDLE
> LET (name of desired lover) BE MINE.
> SO MOTE IT BE!

Fruit Spells

To cause pangs of love in your beloved, stick pins into a lime as your recite his or her name aloud.

For a long and happy marriage, insert eleven golden pins into an apple. Bless it in the sacred name of Frey, and then sleep with it under your pillow the night before your wedding. (Wearing an orange blossom as a bridal flower will also help to ensure a joyful marriage, fruitfulness, and eternal love.)

According to folklore, the fruit of the mandrake (known in some cultures as "love apples") can cause a man to fall in love with a woman if she gives it to him on Saint Agnes' Eve.

To Induce Love Between a Married Couple

According to a grimoire of medieval European folk magick, powder some periwinkle or ground ivy when the moon is in the sign of the Bull. Wrap it in a houseleek and take at meals.

To Attract a Wealthy Husband

Rub your body for five days with the oil of turmeric—the root of an East Indian plant (Curcuma longa) of the ginger family. This love spell is performed mainly by women in Orissa; however, it can also be used by a man to attract a wife.

To Bring Back an Errant Lover

Burn laurel leaves on Saint Valentine's Day as you repeatedly chant out loud the name of your lover.

To Make a Man Love You

On Midsummer's Eve, pick a red rose, carefully wrap it in
a piece of white silk or satin, and keep it hidden in a dark,
undisturbed place until Christmas Day. Open the silk, and
if the rose is still intact, wear it in your buttonhole. The first
gentleman who admires it will fall desperately in love with
you and become your husband.

An Old German Spell to Bring Back a Lover

If you wish to retain the affections of a lover who has proven untrue to you, light three candles at the wrong ends and thrice repeat the Paternoster.

Marriage Spell From Scotland

Place an ivy leaf (the symbol of marriage and fidelity) between your breasts and recite the following magickal incantation:

IVY LEAF, I LOVE YOU TRUE,
IN MY BOSOM I HOLD YOU.
THE FIRST YOUNG MAN WHO SMILES AT ME
MY FUTURE HUSBAND HE SHALL BE.

Voodoo Love Spell

To make a powerful Voodoo love power, burn a handful of dried roses on a night when the moon is full, and mix the ashes with the powdered skull of a serpent and a pinch of white sand.

On a Friday night (when the power of Erzulie is the most intense), make a small wax doll to symbolize the man or woman from whom you desire love. Mix a small bit of hair, blood, or powdered fingernail clippings from the intended lover with the wax to give the doll power. (To make it even stronger, dress it in a piece of fabric obtained from the clothing of the person whom the doll is made to represent.)

After the doll has been made, light a tall, pink candle. Tie a red string around the doll and then sprinkle a bit of the love powder over it and say:

O ERZULIE, LADY OF LOVE
LET THIS DOLL BE (name).
LET HIS (her) HEART BEAT FOR ME
UNTIL I RELEASE HIM (her)
FROM THIS SPELL.

Pour some champagne on the ground as a libation to the loa, give thanks to her and then wrap the love doll in a white cloth and keep it safe in a secret place.

To break the love spell, untie the red string from the wax doll to release the lover from the power of Erzulie and then burn the doll in a forest clearing when the moon is waning.

To Make a Lover Come to You

Stick two silver pins through the middle of a red candle at midnight. Concentrate on your lover and repeatedly chant his or her name out loud. When the candle burns down to the pins, your lover will arrive. (This, according to a modern grimoire of folk magick.)

To Reclaim the Affections of a Lost Lover

Thrust two pins or needles through the wick of a burning candle as you say out loud the name of the lover whose affections you desire.

Tulip Spell

Write the name of the man or woman from whom you desire love next to your name on a tulip bulb (sacred to Venus, the goddess of love). Plant the bulb in the earth and when the tulip blooms, so shall your love.

The Willow Knot Spell

To win the love of a young lady, according to old Gypsy Witch lore, a young man must go into the woods on Saint John's Day (Midsummer) and find some willow twigs that have grown together into a knot. With a sharp, white- handled knife, he must cut the twigs, put them into his mouth, and repeat the following incantation with his eyes closed:

WILLOW TREE, WILLOW TREE
GIVE ME THE LUCK OF THINE,
THEN (name of loved one)
SHALL FOREVER BE MINE.

The Spell of Nine

To make any person desire you, perform this spell at nine o'clock on a night when the moon is in Taurus. Write the full name of the man or woman you love, along with yours, nine times on a tall pink candle. Anoint the candle with a fragrant mixture of rose water and honey, light it, and let it burn for nine minutes, every night at nine o'clock for nine nights in a row.

On the ninth night, after the candle has been extinguished, wrap it tightly in a piece of pink silk. Tie it securely with a pink ribbon and bury it in a churchyard. (It is very important that you bury it without anyone seeing you, or else the spell will lose its effectiveness.)

To Restore a Lover's Affections

Mix a pinch of your powdered fingernail clippings with red wine and then serve it to your unsuspecting lover on a night when the moon is in a waxing phase.

Ancient Gypsy Love Spell

Upon an onion or garlic bulb, write the name of the man or woman you wish to have as your lover. Plant it in a red clay pot; and as you do this, repeat the person's name aloud. Every day at sunrise and at sunset you must water the pot and recite the following magickal incantation over it: AS THIS ROOT GROWS, SO SHALL THE LOVE OF (name of your beloved) GROW FOR ME.

To Gain the Love of Another

At midnight when the waxing moon is in either the sign of Libra or Taurus, cast into a blazing hearth fire a pinch of rosemary, dragon's blood, two rose petals, and any of the following dried roots: mandrake, serpentaria, ginseng. As the magickal herbs burn, relax and fill your mind with romantic visions of the man or woman from whom you desire love and affection. Chant out loud his or her name until the fire burns itself completely out.

If You Wish to Attract a Lover, But Have No Specific Person in Mind

At sunset on a Friday when the moon is in a waxing phase, cast any three of the following herbs into a blazing hearth fire (or bonfire, if outdoors): basil, catnip, coriander, ginger, jasmine, powdered juniper berries, lavender, lovage, rosemary, rose petals, violets, or yarrow. As the herbs burn, recite the following magickal incantation:

> MY TRUE LOVE'S FACE I'VE YET TO SEE.
> I KNOW NOT WHAT HIS (HER) NAME MAY BE
> BUT SOON HIS (HER) HEART WILL BEAT FOR ME.
> COME HITHER, MY LOVE.
> SO MOTE IT BE!

Oriental Love Spell

Enchant a shang-luh root by anointing it on a Friday night with either rose or lotus oil, and then (by the light of a red human-shaped candle) recite the following magickal chant thirteen times over the root while concentrating upon a mental image of the person from whom you desire affection:

> O GOD AND GODDESS UP ABOVE
> SEND DOWN TO EARTH YOUR RAYS OF LOVE.
> WITH MAGICK IN THIS MOONLIT HOUR
> BLESS THIS ROOT OF LOVE WITH POWER.
> AIZEN-MYO-O, KIVAN-NON
> AIZEN-MYO-O, KIVAN-NON
> SO MOTE IT BE!

Before the sun rises, bury the enchanted root near the entrance of your beloved's home where he or she will pass by it often and become bewitched by its powerful vibrations of love.

You may also powder the shang-luh root and sprinkle it in a circle around the house of your intended lover. This method works just as effectively.

(PLEASE NOTE: Shang-luh root, a ginseng-like herb, has long been used by Chinese sorcerers as a powerful love-potion ingredient. If you are unable to obtain a shang-luh, you may use a ginseng root in its place.)

Spell of Desire

To make a man desire you sexually, write his full name with yours upon a crimson phallus-shaped candle when the waxing moon enters the sign of Scorpio. Anoint the candle with musk oil, light it, and repeat the following magickal incantation three times:

CRIMSON CANDLE, BRIGHT WITH FIRE
BEWITCH (man's full name) WITH DESIRE!

Close your eyes and visualize the man of your desires making love to you. Continue the erotic visualization until the candle burns itself completely out.

Love Poppets

A Love Poppet is a cloth doll, similar to the popular Voodoo doll, but used by Witches in white magick spells for love and romance.

To make a Love Poppet, you will need two pieces of cloth (equal in size), a pair of scissors, a needle, some thread, ink or paint, and magickal herbs with which to stuff the doll.

On a night of the new moon, concentrate on the man or woman whom the Love Poppet will represent and draw the outline of the person on one of the pieces of cloth. Place it over the other piece of cloth and then carefully cut along the outline with scissors to make two identical doll patterns. With a needle and thread, sew together the two pieces of cloth along the seams but leave the seam at the top of the doll's head open for stuffing.

The next step is to draw the person's facial features, characteristics (such as a mustache, beard, glasses, hair, etc.) and his or her own astrological symbol on the torso of the Love Poppet with ink or paint in the individual's favorite color(s), if that is known. If you are unsure, use red or pink—the colors of passion and love.

Using mugwort, feverfew, sorrel (or any other herb ruled by Venus, the planet of Love), stuff the Love Poppet until it is completely full. (For a complete listing of the herbs associated with love, passion, and romance, see Chapter 5: The Herbs of Love.) After this has been done, sew shut the opening at the top of the doll's head to prevent the magickal herbs from falling out.

The Love Poppet is now ready to be used to draw love into your life.

Love Poppet Spell

On a Friday when the moon is in a waxing phase, lay the Love Poppet on the center of the altar between two pink candles. (Be sure, as you stand before the altar, that you are facing East.) Anoint the candles with some rose oil, and then light them. Sprinkle the Love Poppet with a bit of salted water to consecrate it, and say:

> WITH THIS SALT AND WATER
> I CONSECRATE THEE
> AS A POSITIVE AND POTENT
> TOOL OF LOVE MAGICK.

Pick up your athame with your right hand. Touch the Love Poppet with the tip of the blade to charge it with magickal power as you say:

> IN THE DIVINE NAME OF VENUS
> AND BY HER DIVINE POWERS
> I CHARGE THEE WITH LOVE-DRAWING MAGICK.
> SO MOTE IT BE.

Pick up the Love Poppet and hold it in your hands. As you gaze at it, concentrate on the affections of the man or woman whom the Poppet represents, and direct your love energy into the Poppet. Recite your beloved's name nine times out loud, shouting his or her name loudly on the ninth recitation.

Return the Love Poppet to the center of the altar and tie a red ribbon (symbolizing love) around its body and say:

> WITH RIBBON OF RED
> THIS SPELL I BIND.
> TRUE LOVE AND STRONG LOVE

MAY (name) AND I FIND.
SO MOTE IT BE.

Place your athame on top of the Love Poppet. Extinguish the candles and leave the doll on the altar for three weeks.

After the ritual has been completed, wrap the Love Poppet in a white satin or silk cloth, leaving the ribbon tied to it, and keep it in a safe and secret place where it will never be disturbed.

To Reverse a Love Poppet Spell

Untie the ribbon from the Poppet, remove the magickal herbs of love, and then burn the doll as you recite the following words:

BY THE DIVINE POWERS
OF THE GODDESS OF LOVE
I NOW REMOVE THIS SPELL.
LET (name) LOVE ME NO MORE.
SO MOTE IT BE.

Mix the ashes with the herbs, and then bury the mixture in the ground at midnight when the moon is in a waning phase.

In the event that the person whom the Love Poppet represents should pass on to the spiritual plane, the doll should be immediately wrapped in a black cloth and buried, along with the person, if possible. If this cannot be done, then burn the Love Poppet when the moon is waning and bury the ashes under the shadow of an oak tree.

3

Love Charms

Love amulets (commonly called "love charms") are material objects which are used by Witches as magickal tools to inspire love and romance, reunite parted lovers, attract a spouse, prevent a love affair from breaking up, etc. Other types of amulets are used to avert danger, protect against negative influences such as the Evil Eye, attract good luck, and stimulate good health.

Almost anything may be used as an amulet—a brightly colored gemstone, a religious figurine, a root, a flower, or a bone. Amulets can be carried in the hand or in a pocket, worn as jewelry, buried in the earth, or secretly placed somewhere within a house, a barn, or even a car. They may be bought, found, or made by hand, and also painted or inscribed with magickal words of power or symbols.

The use of amulets is universal among nearly every culture, and is probably most familiar in the form of a rabbit's foot, four-leaf clovers, horseshoes, birthstone rings, and lucky pennies.

Another type of amulet is the charm bag—a small leather, silk, or flannel pocket filled with various magickal things, and worn or carried for protection or attraction. Charm bags used in love magick are called "love bags" or "mojos." In the southern region of the United States they are known as "hoodoo hands," "tricks," and "tricken bags." Native American Indians call them "medicine bundles," and in Africa they are given the name "gris-gris."

A charm bag filled with magickal herbs, leaves, flowers, or roots is known as an "herbal love amulet" or a "Witches' sachet."

Amulet Consecration Ritual

Before using any love amulet, it is absolutely imperative that it be cleansed of any evil or negative vibrations, and then properly blessed in the name of Venus, Aphrodite, or any other goddess or god of love. (For a complete listing of love deities, see Chapter 9: Goddesses of Love, and Chapter 10, Gods of Love.)

The following ritual should take place on a Friday night when the moon is full. You may work either skyclad (nude) or in a white robe, whichever way you feel most comfortable. (Please note—Before performing this ritual, you should ritually bathe in water scented with rose oil or lavender, clear your mind of all negative thoughts or inhibitions, and concentrate upon romantic images and loving feelings.)

To ritually cleanse the amulet, place it on an altar between two white candles. (Be sure you are facing East. Use a compass if you are not exactly sure.) Place the following things upon the altar: a chalice of clear rainwater, a dish of seasalt, a pink or red votive candle, a censer of incense (rose, jasmine, sandalwood, or vanilla-scented), and any of the following love-attracting candle anointing oils: frankincense, jasmine, lavender, or rose.

Starting at the East point of the circle, scribe a circle in a clockwise direction around the altar and yourself to create a sacred space in which to work your love magick. Anoint and light the two white candles, and then light the incense. Pour the salt from the dish into the chalice of water, and then close your eyes for a few minutes and imagine a white light of Goddess energy surrounding your body, shining brighter and growing in size until it fills the entire magick circle.

Starting in the East, sprinkle the salted water onto the circle in a clockwise direction to ritually purify it. As you sprinkle the water, say:

I CONSECRATE THIS MAGICK CIRCLE
BY THE ANCIENT AND MYSTICAL ELEMENTS
OF EARTH, WATER, FIRE, AND AIR.
LET ALL EVIL SPIRITS
BE CAST FORTH HENCEFROM!
LET ALL NEGATIVE VIBRATIONS
BE CAST FORTH HENCEFROM!
LET ALL IMPURITIES AND HINDRANCES
BE CAST FORTH HENCEFROM!
AND LET ALL THAT IS POSITIVE,
LOVING, AND GOOD
ENTER HEREIN.
BLESSED BE THIS MAGICK CIRCLE
IN THE NAME OF THE LOVE GODDESS VENUS
(or Aphrodite, Ishtar, Freya, etc.).
SO MOTE IT BE!

Return the chalice to the altar and then anoint and light
the pink candle as an offering to the love goddess. If you
desire, you may now paint or carve onto the amulet magickal words, names of power, or symbols. When you are
finished, wrap the amulet in a piece of silk or linen, and
then anoint it with a bit of the oil. (If you are working with
an amulet in the form of a charm bag, tie the open end of
the bag securely shut with a piece of cord or string before
anointing it.) Take the amulet in both hands, folded as in
prayer, and pass it through the smoke of the incense three
times in a clockwise direction as you say:

I CONSECRATE THEE AS A TOOL OF
    WHITE MAGICK
AND I CHARGE THEE WITH MIGHTY
    LOVE ENERGY
IN THE DIVINE NAME OF VENUS*
(or Aphrodite, Ishtar, Freya, etc.)

AND BY THE POWER OF THE FOUR
    ELEMENTS.
SO MOTE IT BE!

After the amulet has been blessed, it must be "sealed" either by a drop of candle wax, a kiss, or a drop of blood from your pricked right thumb. The ritual is now ready to be closed. Give thanks to the Goddess, and then, once again starting in the East, uncast the circle in a counterclockwise direction, using a consecrated athame, ceremonial sword, magick wand, or even the tip of your index finger. Extinguish the two white altar candles but allow the pink or red votive to burn itself out.

Once a charm bag or herbal amulet has been created and charged with Goddess power, it should never again be opened. (Not even by the Witch who made it!) To do so would cause it to lose its magickal power. It should also never be touched by anyone except the person for whom the amulet has been made.

In the unfortunate event that the possessor of the charm bag or amulet should pass on to the spiritual plane or decide that he or she has no further use of the amulet, it should be immediately burned or buried deep in the ground.

Amulets and Gemstones

ROSE AMULET
To attract love or passion, wear a rose of the appropriate magickal color in your hair (if you're a woman) or in your lapel (if you're a man): red for passionate love affairs; pink for romance; white for true love; yellow for tender love or to arouse jealous feelings in a love partner.

WISHBONE AMULET
Save the turkey wishbone from a Yule feast and nail it over the front door of your home on New Year's Day to bring a new lover into your life.

SANTERIA LOVE AMULET
Sew five pumpkin seeds into a small bag of yellow or white cotton. Anoint the bag with a drop of honey, and then bless it in the name of Oshun, the goddess of love, marriage, and fertility. Carry the bag in your pocket or purse as a magickal amulet to draw love.

TURMERIC AMULET
Carry five pieces of turmeric in your pocket or purse as an amulet to attract a lover or a spouse.

TREE AMULETS
The following trees are sacred to various love deities, and any of their parts (twigs, leaves, roots, berries, etc.) can be worn or carried as a powerful love- drawing amulet: apple (sacred to Aphrodite); apricot (sacred to Venus); elder (sacred to Freya); myrrh (sacred to Aphrodite); myrtle (sacred to Aphrodite, Astarte, Hathor, and Venus); palm (sacred to Aphrodite); quince (sacred to Aphrodite and Venus); sycamore (sacred to Hathor).

APPLE AMULET
The apple is used in many Voodoo love charms, and is also a love-drawing amulet in the folklore of the Danish, English, and Germans.

ARROW AMULET
Sleeping on an arrow extracted from a body acts as a powerful love charm, according to Pliny, a well-known Roman author of the first century. (The arrow is a symbol sacred to many gods of love, including Cupid, Eros, and Kama.)

VENUS PENTACLE
Wear a consecrated Venus Pentacle on a silver chain or a braided necklace of green and red threads as a magickal talisman to bring passion and romance into your life. The Venus Pentacle (which can easily be obtained at most occult supply shops and mail order catalogues) also works well for those who desire a loving marriage mate.

LEMON PEEL AMULET
With a consecrated athame, cut out a heart-shaped piece from the peel of a lemon. Let it dry in the sun for seven days, and then carry it in your pocket or purse as a love-drawing amulet.

RUNESTONE AMULET
Carry the rune sign "Lagu" in your pocket or purse to draw more love into your life, or place it in a pink silk amulet bag along with catnip herb, rose quartz, amethyst, and pink tourmaline gemstones, and secretly rub the bag when you are in the presence of the man or woman whom you wish to be your lover.

TULIP BULB AMULET
Carry a tulip bulb as a magickal amulet to bring love into your life. You can also wear a tulip bulb on a necklace or

sleep with one under your pillow at night to attract a new lover, increase your sex appeal, or induce romantic dreams.

GOLDEN KEY AMULET
Wear a consecrated golden key on a chain as an amulet to attract a lover or a soulmate. (The key is a symbol sacred to Frigga, the Norse goddess of love, and the patroness of marriage.)

LOVE GODDESS AMULET
A locket containing the image of the love-goddess Venus (or any other deity of love) attracts love and passionate feelings when worn as a magickal amulet on a chain around the neck.

SEASHELL AMULET
Wear a necklace of seashells as an amulet to attract a lover.

PEBBLE AMULET
Water-worn pebbles were regarded as powerful love charms in the Torres Straits. Wear a holed pebble on a string or chain like a necklace, or carry one in your pocket or purse to transmit your love vibrations and to attract a soulmate.

QUARTZ AMULET
Wear or carry a rutilated quartz (also known as "Venus hair stone" and "Cupid's arrows") as a magickal amulet to attract love.

TOPAZ AMULET
Wear a topaz gemstone to attract love or to ensure fidelity. A topaz engraved with the image of a falcon is said to attract a wealthy husband when worn by an unmarried woman.

AMETHYST AMULET
An amethyst works as a powerful love-drawing amulet when worn by one born under the sign of Taurus or Gemini.

DIAMOND AMULET
Wear a diamond amulet to reconcile a broken love affair or to ensure faithfulness in a relationship.

TO ENCHANT A WEDDING RING
Place the ring in a cauldron filled with red wine. Add the following: one leaf from an oak tree, two willow leaves, and three bay leaves. Using the tip of an athame, inscribe the name of the man or woman from whom you desire love on a piece of heart-shaped red wax and put it into the cauldron. Cover it tightly and leave the cauldron on the sill of a window from crescent moon to full moon. Remove the ring from the cauldron and wear it as a love-drawing amulet on a gold chain around your neck.

MOONSTONE AMULET
Wear a ring of moonstone (dedicated to the love-goddess Aphrodite) to attract a soul mate, inspire tender passions, or to protect a love. The powers of moonstone (also known as the "Stone of Love") are extremely potent when it is worn or carried by persons born under the moon-ruled sign of Cancer.

JADE BUTTERFLY AMULET
A carved jade butterfly is a powerful love-drawing amulet. (In China, this amulet is given to brides by their husbands as a symbol of eternal love.)

GEMSTONE AMULETS
Wear an emerald or a lodestone (sacred to both Venus and Aphrodite) on a Friday to attract or strengthen love. Wear

a star sapphire, ruby, beryl, or turquoise as an amulet to inspire love and romance.

COPPER BRACELET AMULET
To attract a lover or to enhance your sexuality, wear a copper bracelet. (Copper is the metal sacred to the love-goddess Venus.)

CORAL AMULET
Wear or carry a piece of pink coral as an amulet to attract love.

Mojos and Charm Bags

TO MAKE A MOJO LOVE BAG FOR A LADY WHO DESIRES THE AFFECTIONS OF
A CERTAIN MAN:

Put into a small red flannel or chamois drawstring bag a small heart carved out of a piece of red wax and containing the hair and/or fingernail clippings from both the woman and the gentleman whom she desires, a pinch of dried passion flowers, an orris root, vervain, and love-drawing powder. (To make love-drawing powder, place into a mortar: one ounce of powdered sandalwood, ¼ teaspoon of cinnamon, one teaspoon of sweet basil, and one teaspoon of dried and powdered rose petals. Using a pestle, powder all of the ingredients and then add two drams of red rose oil. After the oil has been completely blended with the herbs, slowly add four ounces of talc.)

On a Friday night when the moon is in a waxing phase, place the mojo bag in the center of the altar between two red candles. Light the candles and place a cup of anointing oil and an incense burner filled with smoldering patchouli incense before the mojo bag.

After anointing the bag with any of the following love oils: lavender, lotus, patchouli, or rose, take the mojo in both hands and pass it through the smoke of the incense three times in a clockwise motion as you chant:

HEART OF RED WAX AND PASSION FLOWER,
ORRIS, VERVAIN, AND SWEET LOVE POWDER
IN THIS SACRED VENUS HOUR
BEWITCH THIS MOJO WITH LOVE POWER.
SO MOTE IT BE.

The mojo love bag should be worn near the heart (suspended on a white string or gold chain, or pinned to the inside of a bra) and anointed once a week on a Friday with the same love-attracting oil that was used during the ritual.

It is important that the woman who wears the mojo love bag fixes her thoughts on her intended lover and chants his name often. She should also have strong faith and patience, for although the mojo is a potent form of love magick, not all desires materialize immediately.

TO MAKE A MOJO LOVE BAG FOR A MAN WHO DESIRES THE AFFECTIONS OF A CERTAIN LADY:

Put into a small red flannel or chamois drawstring bag a pinch of basil (the herb of love), rosebuds, a serpentaria root, the birthstones of both the man and the woman whom he desires, a pinch of catnip, and love-drawing powder. (See previous mojo spell for love-drawing powder recipe.)

On a Friday night when the moon is in a waxing phase, place the mojo bag in the center of the altar between two pink candles. Light the candles and then place a cup of rose oil and an incense burner filled with smoldering patchouli incense before the mojo bag.

After anointing the bag with a few drops of the oil, take the mojo in both hands and pass it through the smoke of the incense three times in a clockwise motion as you chant:

BLESSED BE THIS CHARM OF LOVE
WITH GODDESS POWER FROM ABOVE.
SO MOTE IT BE.

The mojo love bag should be worn on a white string or gold chain around the neck, or carried in a pocket. It is very important that the man who uses the mojo love bag fixes his thoughts on his intended lover and chants her name often.

To keep the magick of the mojo strong and to prevent negative influences and vibrations from hindering its powers, it is essential that the bag be anointed once a week on a Friday with the same rose oil that was used during the ritual.

LOVE GRIS-GRIS: A love gris-gris is the Vodoun version of the mojo love bag, and is used in the same way to attract the affections of the opposite sex. To make a love gris-gris, sew into a bag of red silk a magickal mixture of cloves, juniper berries, a small piece of beryl, three red feathers, and an orris root which has been crushed between two sandstones. By the light of a red candle, anoint the gris-gris bag with a mixture of rosewater and pink champagne, and then wear it pinned to an undergarment next to your skin to attract a lover.

TO ATTRACT A LOVER: According to Hoodoo magick, carry any of the following dried roots in a small charm bag of chamois leather or red cloth: Adam and Eve root, Beth root, ginseng root, John the Conqueror root, mandrake root, orris root.

TO MAKE ANOTHER DESIRE YOU: Wear over your heart a charm bag containing a heart-shaped amulet of pink wax, made on a Friday and scented with lemon, musk or patchouli.

NATIVE AMERICAN CHARM BAG: Fill a buckskin bag with apple seeds and cattail pollen, and carry or wear it to attract a lover.

TO DISPEL THE PAIN OF UNREQUITED LOVE: Carry vervain in your right pocket or in a consecrated charm bag worn over your heart.

TO REUNITE PARTED LOVERS: Find a dead newt (a creature ruled by Venus) and powder it by the light of a waning moon. Place the powder in a small leather pouch with lemon verbena leaves, a diamond (or diamond ring), and a small lock of hair from each of the estranged lovers.

Tie up the end of the pouch with a red cord, and then carry
or wear it as a magickal charm bag.

(IMPORTANT REMINDER: Be sure to use a newt that is al-
ready dead. Never kill any living creature for magickal
purposes!)

VENUS CHARM BAG: By the light of a pink candle,
place into a red flannel drawstring bag a handful of dried
apple peels, some rose petals, and two feathers from a
white dove. Anoint the bag with apple blossom oil, and
bless it in the name of the love-goddess Venus. Tie the end
of the bag securely, and then carry or wear it to attract love.

Magick Love Squares

TO MAKE ONESELF BELOVED BY A MAN: Using red ink or blood from your finger, write the following magick square on a heart-shaped piece of jasmine-perfumed paper, and then secretly mail it to the man from whom you desire love:

```
Q  E  B  H  I  R
E  R  A  I  S  A
B  A  Q  O  L  I
H  I  O  L  I  A
I  S  L  I  A  C
R  A  I  A  C  A
```

TO MAKE ONESELF BELOVED BY A WOMAN: Using red ink or blood from your finger, write the following magick square on a heart-shaped piece of rose-scented paper, and then secretly mail it to the woman from whom you desire love:

```
E  F  E  H  A
F           L
E           Q
H           A
A  L  Q  A  S
```

TO BE BELOVED BY YOUR SPOUSE: Write the following magick love square on a square piece of copper, and then touch your mate on the bare skin with it when the moon is in a waxing phase:

```
D  O  D  I  M
O           I
D           D
I           O
M  I  D  O  D
```

TO OBTAIN THE LOVE OF A WIDOW (OR WIDOWER): Write the following magick love square on a pink, heart-shaped piece of paper, using either red ink or blood from your pricked right thumb, and then secretly mail it to the widowed woman or man whose affections you desire:

```
E  L  E  M
L        E
E        L
M  E  L  E
```

TO BE BELOVED BY A RELATIVE: Write the following magick love square on a piece of white parchment. Name aloud the person from whom you wish platonic love, and then carry the square in your pocket or purse:

```
M  O  D  A  H
O  K  O  R  A
D  O     O  D
A  R  O  K  O
H  A  D  O  M
```

TO OBTAIN THE PLATONIC LOVE OF A FRIEND: Write the following magick love square on a piece of white parchment when the moon is in a waxing phase. Say thrice aloud the name of the friend from whom you desire love, and then wear the square on a white string around your neck:

```
I  A  L  D  A  H
A  Q  O  R  I  A
L  O  Q  I  R  F
D  R  I  I  D  E
A  I  R  D  R  O
H  A  F  E  O  N
```

TO KNOW THE SECRETS OF LOVE: Write the following magick love square on a piece of parchment when the moon is full:

```
C  E  D  I  D  A  H
E                    A
D                    D
I                    I
D                    D
A                    E
H  A  D  I  D  E  C
```

Light a pink votive candle. Place your right hand over the magick love square and concentrate upon whatever love secret you wish to know until the candle has burned itself out. Anoint the square with a drop of rose oil, place it under your pillow, and then go to sleep. The answer you seek shall be revealed to you in a dream.

4

Ancient Love Magick

This chapter contains many interesting examples of love magick from ancient times. They are included solely for historic purposes and for the sake of curiosity.

Do not attempt to create or try any of these spells or potions! Many of the ingredients required are dangerous and difficult (if not totally impossible) for the average person to obtain.

In the early days of Witchcraft, most authors of medieval texts were influenced by the Christian Church's anti-Pagan propaganda and, like many others, mistakenly confused the craft of the Old Religion with the practices of sorcery, black magick, and Satanism (which is actually nothing more than a reverse form of Christianity). As a result, many of the old grimoires of magick and Witchcraft became riddled with love spells, potions, and aphrodisiacs calling for various animal (or human) parts and blood; however, such things are never used in modern-day Witchcraft or Wicca.

(PLEASE NOTE: The mutilation or sacrifice of any living creature to work love magick (or any other type of positive magick) is not recommended! The deliberate taking of any life is not only cruel and unnecessary, it is contrary to the Witches' Rede: "An it harm none, do what thou wilt." It is definitely not. the Wiccan way!)

Egyptian Love Knot

To win the affections of a young man, according to an ancient Egyptian magickal papyrus, take a band of linen of sixteen threads (four of white, four of red, four of blue, and four of green) and make them into one band. Stain it with the blood of a hoopoe (an Old World bird, *Upopa epops*, commonly used in ancient Egyptian magick) and then bind it with a drowned scarab beetle wrapped in a piece of byssus (a fine-texture linen used for wrapping mummies). Bind the love knot to the body of the man whom you desire love from, and it will instantly take effect.

Knotting the Cord

During the Middle Ages, it was believed that a man could be made impotent on his wedding day by the powers of a special three-colored cord when thrice-knotted by an evil sorcerer during the marriage ceremony as the couple exchanged their vows.

To break the spell of the cord or to make oneself immune to the knots, according to an ancient grimoire of magick, the man must fill his pockets with salt and then urinate just before entering the church to meet his bride.

Other spell-breaking methods included rubbing wolf fat on the threshold of the marriage chamber, and wearing a groom's gold wedding ring containing the right eye of a weasel.

Frog Bone Amulet (from an ancient grimoire)

Find a *dead* frog—never kill a live one. To do so will bring you bad luck!— and place it on top of an anthill. After the ants have eaten the flesh from the bones, take the heart-shaped bone and wear it on a chain as a love amulet. If you wish to attract the affections of a particular person, wear the heart-shaped bone and stick the hook-shaped one into an article of clothing belonging to your beloved.

Dove's Heart Amulet

According to a very old book of folk magick, the heart of a dove (sacred to the goddess Venus) should be carried as a magickal amulet (or eaten!) to inspire love in a beloved.

Many love spells from the past consisted of the most bizarre and repulsive ingredients (to say the least), as the following two examples prove:

To Make Oneself Beloved

According to Hoodoo practitioners of the southern United States, put a dead frog in an earthen vessel full of small holes and place it on top of an anthill. After the ants have eaten away the skin and flesh of the frog, grind its skeleton into a fine powder. Mix it with red wine, basil, and the blood of a bat, and then throw a pinch of it into the food or drink of the person from whom you desire affections.

A Love Philtre From the Middle Ages

Take the heart of a dove, the liver of a sparrow, the womb of a swallow, and the kidney of a hare, and reduce them to a fine powder. To the love philtre add an equal part of your blood, also dried and powdered. When the moon is in one of the signs of Venus, put some of the love powder into the food or drink of the person from whom you desire love. After they swallow it, they shall be drawn into love.

To Make a Woman Fall Passionately in Love
With a Man

According to an old book of folk spells from England, take three drops of blood from the little finger (pinky) of the man's left hand and secretly put it in a woman's drink on a night when the moon is waxing. Before the moon wanes, she will be madly in love with him and forsake all others.

Black Cat Love Potion

To make a powerful and infallible love potion, according to William Butler Yeats, dry and ground into a powder the liver of a black cat. Mix it with some tea and pour it from a black teapot.

Unicorn Horn Aphrodisiac

According to various legends of the Middle Ages and the Renaissance, the ground horn of the mystical unicorn is a very potent aphrodisiac when mixed together with red wine.

Australian Aphrodisiac

The tribal Australian Aborigines claim that if you powder the testicles of a kangaroo and then sprinkle some of it over the body of your love-mate, it works as a potent aphrodisiac. (This curious method of stimulating sexual desires is similar to the Native American Indian aphrodisiac recipe which calls for the testicles of a beaver.)

Creole Aphrodisiac

To increase the physical activity of making love (or to pro-
long a man's erection), according to the Creole folk-magi-
cians of Louisiana, roast the heart of a hummingbird, grind
it into a powder, and then mix it with ground cubeb
berries, musk oil, ambergris, honey, and the oil from the
seeds of the marshmallow plant. Rub the mixture on the
genitals.

(Roasted hummingbird hearts were also powdered and
then sprinkled over the body of the man from whom the
Witch desired love and affection.)

Toad Venom Aphrodisiac

According to a seventeenth century magickal recipe to "incline men and women to lust": Hang a black toad by the heels for three days and collect the venom as it drops in an oyster shell. When the moon is full, pour the toad venom into a cast-iron cauldron. Add a quart of ale, three marigold flowers, and some rosemary balm. Bring the mixture to a boil, and then remove the cauldron from the heat and allow the brew to cool. To use it as an aphrodisiac, simply rub a bit of it onto the breasts and genitals.

5

Herbs of Love

The following is a list of many of the magickal herbs commonly used by Witches in love spells, passion spells, and
aphrodisiacs:

absinthe	balm
Adam and Eve root	basil
almond	bay laurel
aloes	Beth root

cinnamon
cinquefoil
cloves
coriander
cubeb berries
damiana
dill seed
 dragon's blood
dulse herb
elecampane
fennel seed
five-finger grass
gentian root
heart's ease
hemp seeds
juniper berries
laurel
lavender
lemon
licorice stick herb
lotus
lovage

magnolia
mandrake
mistletoe
myrtle
orange blossoms
orris root
passion flower
patchouli
periwinkle
primrose
quassia chips
Queen Elizabeth root
rose
rose geranium
satyrion root
scullcap
snakeroot
 spikenard
vanilla
verbena root
vervain
violet

Herbs of Venus

According to astrologically minded herbalists of ancient times, Venus (the planet which personifies love and desire) rules all plants and trees that have particularly beautiful flowers (symbolizing Venus as the goddess of love and beauty), red fruits (which are sacred to the love-goddess), and many of the plants governed by the Venus-ruled astrological signs of Taurus and Libra.

The following list contains many of the herbs and trees under the influence of the planet Venus, their uses in folk medicine and spellcraft, and the deities to whom some of the herbs are dedicated.

ADAM AND EVE ROOT
Used in folk medicine to treat bronchial illnesses. As an herb of magick, Adam and Eve root is used mainly in love spells and charms.

ASTER
A magickal plant used in love magick and in Sabbat potpourris. It is sacred to all Pagan gods and goddesses.

BEDSTRAW
Used in folk medicine to treat burns, wounds, internal bleeding, nosebleeds, sore feet, kidney stones, and urinary diseases. As an herb of magick, bedstraw is used in love spells and charms to attract a lover.

BIRTHROOT
Used in folk medicine to treat bronchial problems, coughs, diarrhea, female problems, hemorrhage from the lungs, and pulmonary consumption. As an herb of magick, birthroot is used in love magick and money spells.

BUGLEWEED
Used in folk medicine to treat coughs, diabetes, diarrhea, tuberculosis, and pulmonary hemorrhaging. As an herb of magick, bugleweed has been used in many Gypsy love spells and as a protective charm against werewolves.

BURDOCK
Used in folk medicine to purify the blood, and to treat fever, ringworms, rheumatism, sties, catarrh, gout, impetigo, eye irritations, gonorrhea, syphilis, cancer, skin burns, and ulcers. As a magickal herb, burdock has been used in aphrodisiacs, love magick, spells to ward off negativity and protect against evil, and in charms to protect against serpents and mad dogs. In the southern regions of the United States, necklaces of burdock were often hung around the necks of babies to cure colic.

CATNIP
Sacred to the Egyptian cat-goddess Bast. Used in folk medicine to treat diarrhea, colds, colic, headache, insanity, nervousness, scarlet fever, smallpox, stomach ailments, hives, respiratory ailments, swellings, and to bring on delayed menstruations. As an herb of magick, catnip has been used in cat-magick, healing rituals, love sachets, fertility charms, shape-shifting, and spells to ensure happiness in a home.

COLTSFOOT
Sacred to the goddess Epona. Used in folk medicine to treat coughs, colds, bronchitis, bronchial asthma, pleurisy, throat catarrh, insect bites, inflammations, toothaches, swellings, burns, leg ulcers, and phlebitis. As an herb of magick, coltsfoot leaves have been used in love spells, smoked in a pipe to produce religious visions, and used as a charm to protect horses against sorcery and illness.

COLUMBINE
Used in folk medicine to treat rheumatic aches and pains, jaundice, sore mouth, sore throat, diarrhea, and obstructions of the liver. As an herb of magick, columbine has been used in spells to attract love, return a lost lover, and induce courage.

COWSLIP
Sacred to the goddess Freya and the Virgin Mary. Used in folk medicine to treat burns, wounds, migraine headaches, cramps, insomnia, convulsions, muscular rheumatism, paralytic ailments, and palsy. As an herb of magick, cowslip has been used to heal sickness, to guard houses against unwanted intruders, to increase one's physical charm and beauty, and to locate lost objects or buried treasure.

CROCUS
Sacred to Venus and Aphrodite. A magickal plant used as a vision-invoking incense by the Egyptians of ancient times. The crocus has also been used in spells to attract love and promote peace, and as a Spring Equinox altar decoration.

DAISY
Sacred to Aphrodite, Artemis, Belides, Freya, Venus, Thor, Mary Magdalene, Saint John, and Saint Margaret of Antioch. Used in folk medicine to treat colds, coughs, gout, rheumatism, mucous congestion, inflamed swellings, burns, chest problems, stomach ailments, intestinal problems, catarrh, colic, and also liver, kidney, and bladder problems. As an herb of magick, the daisy has been used in love magick, love divinations, and spells to attract good luck or make fairies appear.

DITTANY
Sacred to Diana, Persephone, and Osiris. Used in folk med-

icine to cure sciatica, snakebites, toothache, epilepsy, worms, and hysteria. Dittany was used by Native American Indians as a stimulant and a nerve tonic, and to treat intermittent fevers. As an herb of magick, dittany is mainly used in astral projections, spirit invocations and love divinations.

ELDER

Sacred to Venus, Freya, Holda, Elle Woman, Hylde-Moer, and many Mother Goddess figures. Used in folk medicine to treat abrasions, chafed skin, sores, burns, ulcers, rheumatism, headache, water retention, fever, painful swellings, and inflammations. As an herb of magick, the elder has been used to break the power of curses, exorcize evil entities, and protect against negative forces and sorcery. Witches and magicians alike have also used the elder in healing rituals and spells to attract good luck, love, and prosperity. The wood of the elder is commonly used to make magick wands. The berries are said to cure insomnia when placed under a pillow. In Bohemia, a spell recited before an elder tree was at one time believed to cure fever. In Italy, elder wood is used to protect a house against thieves as well as to keep serpents at bay. In many parts of England, knots made from elder twigs were carried as charms against rheumatism.

FEVERFEW

Used in folk medicine to treat colic, colds, diarrhea, constipation, indigestion, intestinal worms, and vertigo. As an herb of magick, feverfew is most commonly carried as a charm to attract love and to protect against fever, illness, and accidents.

FIGWORT

Used in folk medicine to treat anxiety, insomnia, skin diseases, fever, intestinal worms, tuberculosis, scabies, hemorrhoids, and open wounds. As an herb of magick, figwort is used as a protective charm to ward off the evil eye.

FLEABANE
Used in folk medicine to treat dysentery, ulcers, and skin irritations. As an herb of magick, fleabane is used in protection spells and exorcism rituals.

FOXGLOVE
Used in folk medicine to treat asthma, fever, insanity, heart palpitations, and neuralgia. As an herb of magick, the foxglove is used for communion with underworld deities, and to protect against ghosts, evil forces, and sorcery.

GERANIUM
Used in folk medicine to treat dysentery, stomach ulcers, intestinal ailments, and headaches. As an herb of magick, the geranium is used in love magick, spells to increase fertility, protection sachets, Sabbat potpourris, and healing rituals.

GOLDENROD
Used in folk medicine to treat ulcers, diphtheria, hemorrhage, dysentery, headache, vomiting, chest pains, fever, boils, convulsions, sore mouth, and diseases of the lungs and kidneys. As an herb of magick, goldenrod has been used as a divining rod to locate buried treasures. It is also used in love divinations and money spells, and carried as a charm to treat rheumatism and to attract good luck to a Witch's house.

GROUNDSEL
Used in folk medicine to treat jaundice, epilepsy, wounds, gout, coughs, nervous disorders, chapped hands, and poor circulation. A medicinal tea made from the flowering plant was used by Native American Indians to treat kidney ail-

ments and to alleviate the pains of childbirth. As an herb of magick, groundsel is carried as a love charm and also as an amulet to protect against toothache.

HEATHER
Sacred to the Egyptian goddess Isis. Used in folk medicine to treat insomnia, gout, rheumatism, coughs, and stomach ailments. As an herb of magick, heather has been used in spells to bring good luck, increase physical attractiveness, spirit conjurations, protection, and weather-working.

HIBISCUS
Used in folk medicine to treat spasmodic problems, itchy skin, and stomach ailments. As an herb of magick, hibiscus has been used in aphrodisiacs, love incenses and sachets, spells of love, and divination.

HUCKLEBERRY
As an herb of magick, the huckleberry has been used to protect against evil entities, break the power of curses and hexes, attract good luck, and make dreams come true.

HYACINTH
Sacred to Hyacinthus, Apollo, and Artemis. Used in folk medicine as a diuretic and a stimulant. As an herb of magick, the hyacinth is used to attract love, guard against nightmares, and cure fascination. It is also used as a patron herb for gay male Witches.

INDIAN PAINTBRUSH
As an herb of magick, the Indian paintbrush is used in all forms of love magick.

IRIS
Sacred to Iris, Horus, Osiris, and Juno. As an herb of magick, the iris is used in purification rituals, love magick, and

spells to induce faith, wisdom, or valor. Its tuberous root, commonly known as orris root, is often dried and ground and added to magickal incenses and protection amulets. (See *ORRIS ROOT*.)

LADY'S MANTLE

Sacred to the Virgin Mary and various Earth Goddesses. Used in folk medicine to treat diarrhea, enteritis, rheumatism, excessive menstruation, stomach ailments, lack of appetite, wounds, and leukorrhea. It came to be known as an important magickal plant back in the sixteenth century upon the discovery that overnight dew collected in the funnel-shaped folds of its semiclosed nine-lobed leaves. Alchemically minded scientists of that time regarded dew as a highly magickal substance, and the plant was soon nicknamed "Alchemilla," meaning the "little magickal one." Lady's mantle is commonly used in sleep sachets and all forms of love magick.

LILAC

A magickal plant used in Voodoo love magick, exorcisms, and spells to protect against negative influences and evil entities.

MAGNOLIA

Used in folk medicine to treat leukorrhea, dyspepsia, constipation, fever, skin diseases, malaria, nicotine addiction, colds, gout, dysentery, and lung and chest ailments. As an herb of magick, magnolia blossoms are used in love spells and placed under the bed of a lover or spouse to keep him or her faithful.

MAIDENHAIR FERN

Sacred to Venus, Dis, and Kupala. Used in folk medicine to treat asthma, coughs, congestion due to colds, hoarseness, catarrhal problems, jaundice, and pleurisy. As an herb of

magick, the maidenhair fern is used in love magick, Goddess invocations, and weather-working.

MOTHERWORT

Sacred to various Mother Goddesses. Used in folk medicine to increase urine flow, prevent miscarriage, and to
treat rabies, asthma, delirium, neuralgia, and heart palpitations. As an herb of magick, motherwort has been used in
healing rituals, counter-magick, and Chinese immortality
spells. The herb has also been used as an all-powerful
charm against evil spirits.

MUGWORT

Sacred to Artemis and Diana, and associated with the legend of Saint John the Baptist. Used in folk medicine to treat
such ailments as poison oak, skin irritations, dysentery, fatigue, hemorrhages, rheumatism, fever, palsy, epilepsy,
gout, and women's diseases. Mugwort is known as "St.
John's plant" in the countries of Holland and Germany,
and according to folk legend, a girdle made of mugwort
was worn by John the Baptist to protect him against harm
in the wilderness. In Germany, mugwort girdles were
worn to protect the wearer for twelve months against black
magick, sickness, evil spirits, and bad luck. In Poitou, they
were worn to prevent backache. As an herb of magick,
mugwort is also used for breaking hexes cast on animals,
counteracting charms, and exorcising spirits of disease.
The magickal powers of mugwort are said to be most potent when the plant is gathered on Saint John's Eve. A sachet filled with the herb offers a traveler protection against
fatigue, sunstroke, poison, wild beasts, mischievous elves,
and unfriendly spirits. Sleeping on a pillow stuffed with
mugwort induces psychic dreams and lets a person view
his entire future. In China during the time of the Dragon
Festival (the fifth day of the fifth moon), mugwort is hung
to keep away evil demons, while in other parts of the

world, a crown made from the sprays of the plant is worn on Midsummer's Eve to protect the wearer against possession by demonic forces. Mugwort is also worn as a charm to increase fertility, arouse sexual desire, cure diseases and insanity, and aid in achieving astral projection. Brewed as a tea, often with lemon balm, mugwort is consumed to aid divination, meditation, and psychic development. Mugwort tea is also used by many Witches as a ceremonial potion for Samhain and Full Moon rituals, and as a wash to cleanse and consecrate crystal balls, magic mirrors, and quartz crystals.

MYRTLE
Sacred to Aphrodite, Artemis, Ashtoreth, Astarte, Diana, Hathor, Marian, and Venus. Used in folk medicine to treat diarrhea, uterine hemorrhages, sore throat, wounds, cuts, bruises, dysentery, fever, nasal congestion, jaundice, scrofula, intestinal worms, scurvy, and cankers of the mouth and throat. As an herb of magick, myrtle is used in love magick, charms to increase fertility, and money spells.

ORCHID
Sacred to Bacchus and Orchis. Used in folk medicine to treat chronic diarrhea, bilious fevers, and irritations of the gastrointestinal canal. As a magickal plant, the orchid is used in love spells, philtres, and rituals to induce psychic powers. Its root (known also as Satyrion Root or Lucky Hand) is commonly used in wish-magick and New Orleans hoodoo magick to attract good luck and success, and for protection against evil, sorcery, and sickness.

ORRIS ROOT
Sacred to Aphrodite, Hera, Iris, Isis, and Osiris. Used in folk medicine to treat bronchitis, coughs, colic, congestion in the liver, sore throat, dropsy and other water retention problems. As an herb of magick, orris root is used in spells

to attract love, keep evil spirits at bay, and to divine the future. (See also *IRIS*.)

PERIWINKLE

Used in folk medicine as a tonic, and to treat diabetes, cramps, scurvy, inflamed tonsils, diarrhea, hysteria, fits, nervous conditions, toothaches, nosebleeds, excessive menstruation, bleeding piles, and hemorrhages. According to herbalists of the eleventh century, periwinkle should only be gathered on the first, ninth, eleventh, and thirteenth night of the month. As an herb of magick, periwinkle has been used to cure "devil-sickness" and demonic possession. It has also been used in love spells, money spells, philtres, and charms to obtain grace or protect against bad spirits, wild beasts, serpents, and poison. In medieval Germany, it was a popular magickal ingredient in immortality spells and potions. When wrapped in a houseleek with worms and taken at meals, periwinkle is said to induce love between a man and a woman. In Italy, its flowers are placed on dead children's coffins or graves as wreaths to protect the soul while on its journey to the afterlife. In Wales, the herb is used by necromancers to make spirits materialize in graveyards. In many parts of Europe it was nicknamed the "sorcerer's violet" because of its strong connection with witchcraft and wizardry.

PRIMROSE

Sacred to the goddess Freya. Used in folk medicine to treat headaches (ordinary and migraine), insomnia, nervous conditions, general weakness, catarrh, mucous congestion, coughs, bronchitis, lung ailments, and skin blemishes. As an herb of magick, the primrose in used in love spells and protection spells, worn as a charm to cure insanity, and planted in Witches' gardens to attract fairies and benevolent spirits.

RAGWORT

Used in folk medicine to speed childbirth, induce abortion, and treat female problems, coughs, nervous disorders, sciatica, gout, arthritis, inflammation of the eyes, cancers, ulcers, poor circulation, speech impediments, sores, venereal infections, and problems of the urinary tract. As an herb of magick, ragwort was used in medieval times to keep evil spirits and demons at bay. The Greeks used it to protect against charms and sorcery, and in Cornwall, it was commonly believed that Witches used stalks of the plant to ride upon in the dark of night. In Ireland, ragwort was associated with fairy-folk and was given the nickname of "fairies' horse"

RASPBERRY

Sacred to Venus. Used in folk medicine to treat dysentery, sore mouths, cankers of the throat, runny noses, wounds, ulcers, scalds, and extreme laxity of the bowels. As an herb of magick, the raspberry is used in love spells, philtres, and aphrodisiacs. The brambles of the plant are used as charms to protect a home against ghosts.

ROSE

Sacred to Venus, Freya, Chloris, Flora, Hathor, Holda, Eros, Cupid, Demeter, Isis, Adonis, Aurora, Aphrodite, and the Virgin Mary. Used in folk medicine to treat sore throat, sprains, headache, dizziness, mouth sores, uterine cramps, toothache, and earache. As an herb of magick, nearly all parts of the rose have been used in love spells, enchantments, and transformations. It was (and still is) believed by many to possess aphrodisiac qualities. Rose oil is used in spells to increase courage. Garlands of rosebuds are used by many modern Witches to decorate their Yule tree, while magickal brews made from the buds are said to cause visions of the future to appear in dreams. In British Columbia, roses were sacred to the Thompson Indians, and were used ritually to "purify" widows and widowers of the ghosts of their deceased mates. Throughout Germany it was believed that roses were guarded by dwarfs and fairies, and unless a person asked their permission before picking a rose, he or she would run the risk of losing a hand or a foot.

STRAWBERRY
Sacred to Freya, Frigga, Venus, and the Virgin Mary. Used in folk medicine to treat inflammations, fainting spells, melancholia, gout, ulcers, jaundice, venereal infections, palpitations of the heart, and diseases of the blood, liver, and spleen. As a magickal plant, the strawberry is used in love spells, philtres, and aphrodisiacs. The leaves of the plant are also carried as a charm or used in herbal amulets to attract good luck.

TANSY
Sacred to the Virgin Mary. Used in folk medicine to treat fevers, sprains, headache, pimples, sunburn, inflamed eyes, stomachaches, cramps, intestinal worms, ulcers, and inflammations of the lungs. As an herb of magick, tansy has been used in spells for invisibility and immortality, and to keep evil ghosts from entering a house. In Sussex, England, tansy leaves were worn in the shoe as a charm against fever. In many parts of Europe, it was worn by women to aid conception and prevent miscarriage.

THYME
Used in folk medicine to treat disorders of the nervous system, depression, insomnia, and epilepsy. As an herb of magick, thyme is used in love spells and divinations, dream-magick, spells to increase strength and courage, and charms against nightmares. Thyme is also used in healing spells, purifications, and rituals to develop extrasensory perception.

TULIP

Used as a magickal plant in all forms of love magick and spells to attract good luck and money. The tulip has also been carried or worn as a charm to protect against bad luck, demonic entities, and the evil eye.

VANILLA

Used in folk medicine to treat malaria. As an herb of magick, the vanilla plant is used in love magick. The beans are used as amulets to improve mental powers, and the purple flowers are used in aphrodisiacs and passion sachets.

VERVAIN

Sacred to Aradia, Cerridwen, Demeter, Isis, Juno, Jupiter, Mars, Mercury, Persephone, Thor, and Venus. Used in folk medicine to induce vomiting, increase perspiration to break fevers, clear the respiratory tracts of mucus, and treat jaundice, dropsy, gout, headache, neuralgia, ophthalmia, intestinal worms, stomach ailments, pleurisy, swelling of the spleen, wounds, ulcers, piles, whooping cough, liver diseases, and rheumatism. As one of the most mystical herbs of magick, vervain has been used in wish-magick, love potions, aphrodisiacs, divinations, charms, incantations, money spells, exorcisms, purifications, and ancient ritual sacrifices. Vervain is said to repel evil ghosts and incubi, protect against all forms of sorcery, enchantments and charms, cure diseases, turn enemies into friends, open locks magickally, protect a home against storms and lightning, and enable one to see into the future. Given the appropriate nickname of "Enchanter's Plant," vervain was used by the ancient Druids in prophecy; the Persians in their worship of the sun; the Romans used it to decorate the altars of Venus and Jupiter; and the Anglo-Saxons carried the plant's root as a charm to cure ulcers. When worn around the neck as a charm, vervain is said to attract good luck and protect the wearer from headaches and the venomous bites of serpents. In the Victorian language of flowers, vervain is the symbol of enchantment.

VIOLETS

Sacred to Venus, Aphrodite, Io, Attis, and the Virgin Mary. Used in folk medicine to induce vomiting and to treat skin abrasions, pulmonary problems, constipation, inflammation of the eyes, spasmodic coughs, cancerous growths (especially in the throat), ague, epilepsy, sleeplessness, pleurisy, jaundice, and quinsy. As an herb of magick, the violet has often been used in aphrodisiacs, love spells, wish-magick, and healing rituals. Violets have also been worn in sachets, herbal amulets, and mojo bags to keep evil spirits at bay, heal wounds, counteract bad luck, and cure insomnia. African violets, also under the influence of Venus, are used in protection spells and Goddess invocations.

WOOD SORREL

Sacred to Saint Patrick and all Triple Goddesses. Used in folk medicine to treat hemorrhages, gout, rheumatism, fevers, catarrhs, urinary disorders, heartburn, and mild liver and digestive problems. As an herb of magick, wood sorrel leaves are commonly used in healing rituals, and carried as charms to protect the heart.

YARROW

Sacred to the Horned God of the Wiccans. Used in folk medicine to treat stomach cramps, lack of appetite, flatulence, gastritis, enteritis, gallbladder and liver ailments, fevers, sprains, internal hemorrhages (particularly in the lungs), nosebleeds, wounds, sores, rheumatism, toothache, gonorrhea, chapped hands, sore nipples (from breastfeeding), and excessive menstrual flow. As an herb of magick, yarrow has been worn as a charm against sorcery, demons, negativity, and ghosts; used in love divinations, I Ching divinations, and exorcisms; and hung in houses on Midsummer's Eve to protect the inhabitants against sickness throughout the ensuing year. Many modern Witches have used yarrow in rituals and brews to increase psychic powers, and the herb is often worn at Pagan handfasting ceremonies to dispel negative influences.

Flowers of Love

In the Victorian language of flowers, the following plants symbolize the various aspects of love:

ACACIA: Platonic love
AMBROSIA: Love returned
BACHELOR'S BUTTONS: Hope in love
BRIDAL ROSE: Happy love
CABBAGE ROSE: Ambassador of love
CAROLINA ROSE: The dangers of love
HONEY FLOWER: Sweet and secret love
HONEYSUCKLE: The bonds of love
LEMON BLOSSOMS: Fidelity in love
LINDEN FLOWER: Conjugal love
LOTUS: Estranged love
MOSS: Maternal love
MYRTLE: Love and fertility
PINK CARNATION: Women's love
PURPLE LILAC: First emotions of love
RED CATCHFLY: Youthful love
RED TULIP: Declaration of love
ROSE: Love and marriage
THORNLESS ROSE: Early attachment
TOOTHWORT: Secret love
YELLOW ROSE: Decrease of love; jealousy
YELLOW TULIP: Hopeless love

6

Love Potions and Aphrodisiacs

Santeria Love Perfume

Add to a bottle of your favorite perfume or cologne, a few drops of musk oil, a pinch of ground coral, cantharides ("Spanish fly"), brown sugar, cinnamon, and rose petals. Shake well and then place the bottle in front of an image of Oshun (the Santeria love-goddess) for five days and nights.

'To attract a lover, rub some of the magickal love perfume on your forehead, breasts, and feet.

Basic Love Potion

Fill a small cauldron or pot with a handful of rosemary leaves, thirteen anise seeds, two cloves, three rose geranium leaves, a tablespoon of honey, and some red wine. Place the cauldron over a fire and bring the brew to a boil. Strain the mixture through a sieve. Add some of the liquid to a glass of wine or fruit juice, and then serve it to the man or woman from whom you desire love.

Gypsy-Witch Love Potion

1 cup water
¼ cup red wine
1 teaspoon fennel
1 teaspoon vervain 3 pinches of nutmeg

Place all ingredients into a cauldron (or small pot) over a fire and bring to a boil. Sit before the cauldron with a pink candle and concentrate on the man or woman from whom you wish love, chanting his or her name out loud for thirteen minutes.

Remove the cauldron from the flames and strain the potion through a cheesecloth. Add a bit of honey to sweeten the potion, and then give it to the one you desire.

(PLEASE NOTE: Be sure to prepare this love potion on a Friday night when the moon is in a waxing phase. If the moon should happen to be in either of the Venus-ruled signs (Taurus or Libra), all the better!)

Love Potion No. 9

9 oz. sweet red wine
9 basil leaves
9 red rose petals
9 cloves
9 apple seeds
9 drops vanilla extract
9 drops strawberry juice
9 drops raspberry juice
ginseng root, cut into
9 equal pieces

By the light of nine pink votive candles, put these nine ingredients into a cauldron on the ninth hour of the ninth day of the ninth month of the year.

Stir the potion nine times with a wooden spoon, each time reciting the following magickal incantation:

> LET THE ONE WHO DRINKS THIS WINE
> SHOWER ME WITH LOVE DIVINE.
> SWEET LOVE POTION NUMBER NINE
> MAKE HIS/HER LOVE FOREVER MINE.

Bring the mixture to a boil and then reduce the heat and let it simmer for nine minutes. Remove the cauldron from the heat and allow the potion to cool off.

Blow nine times upon the potion, bless it in the names of nine love- goddesses, and then strain it through a cheesecloth into a clean container. Cover and refrigerate it until you are ready to serve it to the man or the woman from whom you desire love and affection. (Do not allow anyone other than your beloved to look at, touch, or drink the love potion!)

A word of warning: This potion is extremely potent and

should be used with caution. Its results can be very intense, long-lasting, and often difficult to control or reverse. So please be absolutely sure before you give it to an intended lover that he or she is the right one for you, and vice versa.

Honeymoon Aphrodisiac

On each day of the first thirty days of your marriage, drink a potion of mead mixed with honey to arouse passion and intense sexual desires.

Mandrake Aphrodisiac

To create a powerful aphrodisiac, add a tiny particle of powdered female mandrake leaf to a cup of wine. (Use caution when working with mandrake root, both male and female, for it is a very magickal plant and taken in large doses it can result in delirium or painful death.)

Aphrodisiac Sachet

During a full moon, place an herb mixture of verbena, lemon, serpentaria root, and elder flowers on the center of a square of red felt or cotton. Gather up the ends and tie them together with red wool yarn or cotton twine. Place this powerful sachet under your pillow, or wear it on a string around your neck.

Venus Aphrodisia Wine

Boil two teaspoons of passion fruit juice, two powdered juniper berries, and a pinch of ground dried basil in red wine while chanting:

VENUS WINE BUBBLE AND TURN
PASSION BURN
PASSION BURN

Passion Potpourri

2 oz. violet
2 oz. orris root
1 oz. lovage
½ oz. rose leaf
½ oz. rose petal
1 oz. rosemary
1 oz. tonka bean
½ oz. lemon leaf

Cut and collect the herbs on a dry morning after the dew has dried. Tie the herbs together securely with a red string and hang them to dry in an attic or other warm, dark, airy place. Remove the string after the herbs are dry and brittle, and break them into large coarse pieces. (It is important that the herbs be completely dry, otherwise mold will develop and ruin the potpourri.) Stir all of the ingredients together with a large wooden spoon and then place in a large glass jar, bottle, or jug, and seal with a tight-fitting lid. Keep the potpourri in a cool dark place for three months, removing the lid and stirring the contents with a wooden spoon at least once a week.

Passion Aphrodisiac

Place a handful of the Passion Potpourri into a nylon stocking, muslin or cheesecloth bag and add to your bathwater to increase sexual power.

Passion Sachet

On a night of the waxing moon, place one ounce of the Passion Potpourri in a silk handkerchief. Fill your mind with romantic thoughts as you gather together the corners of the handkerchief and tie them securely with a piece of red velvet. Carry the sachet of Passion Potpourri with you at all times during the day to help guide a lover into your life. At night, place the sachet under your pillow before you go to sleep.

Passion Vision Incense

Burn a pinch of the Passion Potpourri on a hot charcoal block as a magickal incense to receive a psychic vision of your future lovemate.

Love Perfume

Love perfumes have been used since ancient times by nearly every culture around the world.

Although usually worn on the body to attract or keep a lover, love perfumes can also be added to ritual baths to intensify magickal power, stirred into hot wax or tallow to scent and impower homemade candles for love spells, worn as sacred offerings to corresponding love deities, and used to anoint the amulets and talismans of love magick.

The following fragrances are ideal to wear or use as love-drawing perfumes: apple blossom, frankincense, honeysuckle, hyacinth (especially for gay lovers), jasmine, lavender, lemon blossom, myrrh, myrtle, orange blossom, orchid, patchouli, and rose.

To attract a new sex partner or to arouse the sexual desires of your present lover, use any of the following fragrances: lotus, musk, strawberry, vanilla, violet.

To keep your lover faithful to you, wear a bit of magnolia perfume or cologne when making love, or lightly sprinkle a small amount on the sheets of your bed just before sexual activity. (PLEASE NOTE: Apple blossom perfume can also be used just as effectively.)

To reunite parted lovers, any of the following fragrances are recommended: lotus, magnolia, rose.

To attract a marriage partner or a soulmate, wear a bit of apple blossom or orange blossom perfume. These two-sweet fragrances are said to work especially well for women wishing to find a husband. (WARNING: If you are seriously marriage-minded, one fragrance to definitely avoid at all costs is lilac for it is considered to be an extremely unlucky fragrance for lovers.

According to old European folklore, a woman who

wears lilacs (except on May Day) will die a spinster, and if any person should be foolish enough to give a spray of lilacs to his or her betrothed, their marriage engagement will soon be broken off. (You may or may not believe in old superstitions, but why take a chance?)

7

Star Signs of Love

According to most astrology books, each sign of the zodiac is most compatible with certain other ones in the area of love and romance. However, a relationship between two opposite personalities such as a Gemini man and a Capricorn woman (a less than perfect astrological match) can often turn out to be a very beautiful, harmonious, and fulfilling one, provided that both partners are able to accept each other's differences and opposite astrological personality traits. For instance, the youthful-looking and imaginative Gemini can mellow out the Capricorn's dark and often manic moods with his unique wit and sense of humor, and keep her from falling into a dull, boring rut with his love for excitement, travel, and change. On the other hand, the practical, ambitious, and strong-willed Capricorn can stabilize her flighty Gemini mate and offer him a sense of security through her earthiness and love for home and family.

By the same token, two people who are astrologically suited for each other (a Leo and an Aries, for instance) can end up in a disastrous or unhappy relationship if they don't work out their differences and accept each other's faults or weaknesses.

The Twelve Signs of the Zodiac

ARIES (March 21–April 20)
  Symbol: The Ram
  Element: Fire
  Masculine/Positive
  Planetary Rulers: Mars and Pluto
  Most compatible with: Aries, Leo, Sagittarius, and those
    with Moon in Aries.
TAURUS (April 21–May 21)
  Symbol: The Bull
  Element: Earth
  Feminine/Negative
  Planetary Ruler: Venus
  Most compatible with: Taurus, Virgo, Capricorn, and
    those with Moon in Taurus.
GEMINI (May 22–June 21)
  Symbol: The Twins
  Element: Air
  Masculine/Positive
  Planetary Ruler: Mercury
  Most compatible with: Gemini, Libra, Aquarius, and
    those with Moon in Gemini.
CANCER (June 22–July 23)
  Symbol: The Crab
  Element: Water
  Feminine/Negative
  Planetary Ruler: The Moon
  Most compatible with: Cancer, Scorpio, Pisces, and those
    with Moon in Cancer.
LEO (July 24–August 23)
  Symbol: The Lion
  Element: Fire
  Masculine/Positive

Planetary Ruler: The Sun
Most compatible with: Leo, Sagittarius, Aries, and those
   with Moon in Leo.
VIRGO (August 24–September 23)
   Symbol: The Virgin
   Element: Earth
   Feminine/Negative
   Planetary Ruler: Mercury
   Most compatible with: Virgo, Capricorn, Taurus, and
      those with Moon in Virgo.
LIBRA (September 24–October 23)
   Symbol: The Scales
   Element: Air
   Masculine/Positive
   Planetary Ruler: Venus
   Most compatible with: Libra, Aquarius, Gemini, and
      those with Moon in Libra.
SCORPIO (October 24–November 22)
   Symbol: The Scorpion
   Element: Water
   Feminine/Negative
   Planetary Rulers: Mars and Pluto
   Most compatible with: Scorpio, Pisces, Cancer, and those
      with Moon in Scorpio.
SAGITTARIUS (November 23–December 21)
   Symbol: The Centaur-Archer
   Element: Fire
   Masculine/Positive
   Planetary Ruler: Jupiter
   Most compatible with: Sagittarius, Aries, Leo, and those
      with Moon in Sagittarius.
CAPRICORN (December 22–January 19)
   Symbol: The Goat
   Element: Earth

Feminine/Negative
Planetary Ruler: Saturn
Most compatible with: Capricorn, Taurus, Virgo, and
    those with Moon in Capricorn.
AQUARIUS (January 20–February 19)
    Symbol: The Water-Bearer
    Element: Air
    Masculine/Positive
    Planetary Ruler: Uranus
    Most compatible with: Aquarius, Gemini, Libra, and
        those with Moon in Aquarius
PISCES (February 20–March 20)
    Symbol: The Fishes
    Element: Water
    Feminine/Negative
    Planetary Rulers: Jupiter and Neptune
    Most compatible with: Pisces, Cancer, Scorpio, and those
        with Moon in Pisces.

Venus: The Planet of Love

The ancient Romans, Greeks, and Babylonians associated the morning and evening star with Venus, the gracious goddess of love and beauty.

It is the only planet named after a goddess, and its astrological symbol is widely used outside of the astrological sciences to represent the female principle. (The corresponding symbol of the male principle is the planet Mars, named after the lover of Venus in classical mythology.)

The force of Venus is connected with love magick, sex magick, and fertility rites. Copper (the metal assigned to the love goddess by astrologers and alchemists) is said to be useful in astrologically prepared love charms.

In astrology, Venus is traditionally the ruler of love, desire, sexuality, beauty, and relationships in general. It is an essentially beneficent planet, attracting love, harmony, affection, peace, and reconciliation.

The planet Venus in the signs of the zodiac reveals important information about how a person expresses his or her emotions in love and marriage, and its influence varies according to its particular location in a person's horoscope.

VENUS IN ARIES: A person who has Venus in Aries will be competitive, aggressive in his or her emotional self-expression, and passionate in romantic love affairs. However, Venus in the sign of the Ram can often produce impulsive and unstable affections.

VENUS IN TAURUS: A person who has Venus in Taurus will be stable in love, loyal, and emotionally secure. He or she will also be a lover of comfort, beauty, art, and luxury. However, on the negative side, Venus in the sign of the Bull can sometimes produce a jealous and/or possessive nature.

VENUS IN GEMINI: A person who has Venus in Gemini is friendly, witty, talkative, easily bored, and often fickle when it comes to love. The sign of the Twins also indicates curiosity, an intense need for freedom, and the desire to constantly seek out new experiences. Although they are capable of loyalty and devotion, many Venus in Gemini persons possess extremely changeable affections, and find it extremely difficult (if not altogether impossible) to settle down with one love-mate in a permanent romantic relationship.

VENUS IN CANCER: A person who has Venus in Cancer tends to be dignified, unpredictable, extremely sensitive in romantic love affairs, easily hurt, and affectionate (especially toward children). Because Cancer is the maternal sign, women (and even men) with Venus in Cancer are usually very domestic and make excellent mothers and fathers. However, on the negative side, Venus in the sign of the Crab can make a person moody and overly sensitive, and produce unstable emotional reactions.

VENUS IN LEO: A person who has Venus in Leo tends to be proud, sociable, warmhearted, loving, loyal, and generous. He or she may like to show off and be noticed by others. A competitive nature is also a strong possibility. However, the negative side of Venus in the sign of the Lion can produce selfishness, snobbery, jealousy, possessiveness, and an uncontrollable sex drive.

VENUS IN VIRGO: A person who has Venus in Virgo tends to be kind, sympathetic, and extremely fastidious about manners and appearance. He or she may also possess a strong tendency to overanalyze emotions, and criticize loved ones. Most men and women with this particular Venus position never get married because their overanalytic traits and highly critical expectations of a spouse often interfere with the development of a romantic relationship with a love-mate.

VENUS IN LIBRA: A person who has Venus in Libra usually places a great deal of importance on love, marriage, and harmonious social relationships. He or she understands and respects the feelings of others, and also possesses a well-developed sense of justice and fair play where friendships and romantic relationships are concerned. However, the negative side of Venus in the sign of the Scales can be superficial emotional and social values, nervousness, and a quick or uncontrollable temper.

VENUS IN SCORPIO: A person who has Venus in Scorpio possesses intense, passionate emotions and sexual desires, and tends to be proud, artistic, sensitive to the feelings of others, highly sensual (often kinky), and preoccupied with sex. It is common for persons who have Venus in the sign of the Scorpion to be involved in love/hate relationships, and they may possess a secretive, possessive, and/or jealous nature.

VENUS IN SAGITTARIUS: A person who has Venus in Sagittarius possesses a friendly and outgoing nature, idealistic emotions and responses, and a tendency to be outspoken about his or her inner feelings to lovers or spouses. Persons with Venus in the sign of the Archer seek honesty and beauty, and are usually dissatisfied in a love relationship unless they settle down with a mate who shares the same religious and/or philosophic beliefs. The negative side of Venus in Sagittarius can result in unrealistic romantic idealism, religious prejudice, and a tendency to be insensitive to the feelings and/or emotional needs of loved ones.

VENUS IN CAPRICORN: A person who has Venus in Capricorn tends to be refined, intelligent, loyal, and emotionally stable. He or she appreciates the finer things in life, desires to feel superior, and often chooses to marry a wealthy partner in order to achieve emotional security through material status and wealth. Although proud and reserved in public, persons who have Venus in this particular position can be quite sensual (even downright kinky) behind closed doors. If they marry at a young age, they are usually attracted to older mates; and if they marry later in life, they usually settle down with younger partners. The negative side of Venus in the sign of the Goat can be emotional coldness, greed, materialism, stubbornness, snobbery, reclusiveness, paranoia, and manic depression.

VENUS IN AQUARIUS: A person who has Venus in Aquarius tends to be friendly, loyal, outgoing, eclectic, and intellectual. He or she may desire new experiences, mental stimulation, and personal freedom. Jealousy and possessiveness are not typical Venus in Aquarius traits; however, many persons who have Venus in this particular position find marriage or permanent love relationships to be too confining. The negative side of Venus in the sign of the Water-Bearer can be fickleness and eccentric or promiscuous sexual behavior.

VENUS IN PISCES: A person who has Venus in Pisces tends to be compassionate, sympathetic, romantic, understanding, and sensitive to the feelings of others. He or she may possess a strong fear of rejection by a lover or spouse. The negative side of Venus in the sign of the Fish can be neurotic tendencies, emotional hypersensitivity, laziness, and extreme emotional dependence on loved ones.

IMPORTANT NOTE: **To find out in which sign of the zodiac your planet Venus is in, consult a professional astrologer or send your name, address, and full birthdate (along with $1.00 and a self-addressed stamped envelope) to: GOLDEN ISIS (Dept. L.M.), P.O. box 525, Fort Covington, NY 12937**

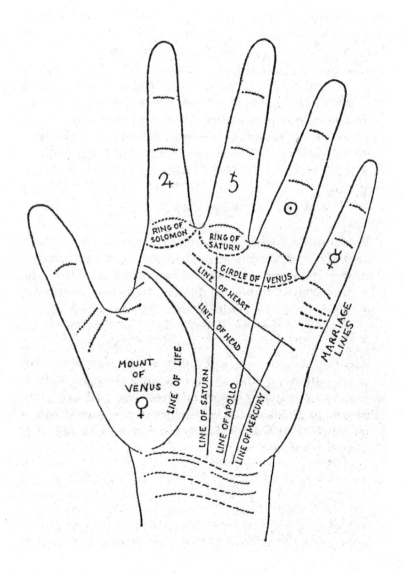

8

Love in the Palm of Your Hand

The Lines of Love

A clear and unbroken line of heart reveals loyalty and a strong love for family.

If the line of heart starts between the first and second finger, it reveals that you are a sensual lover. If it starts between the second and third finger, it indicates that you possess a negative attitude toward love and/or marriage.

Love and passion are greatly increased when a double line of heart is present.

An absent line of heart reveals that you have a tendency to be an extremely selfish lover.

If the lines of heart, head, and life are connected at the beginning, it reveals that you are an extremely loving person, but you will experience unhappiness and disappointments in marriage.

A high line of heart reveals a warm and affectionate nature. If it starts low and runs in a straight line, it reveals that you hide your love and are secretive about your feelings.

A wavy line of heart denotes uncertainty in matters of love and romance.

A line of heart with small bars that cut through from beginning to end indicate that you will be greatly disappointed by your lover or spouse.

A line of heart that ends in a fork denotes a marriage that will end in divorce.

A line of heart that has a tassled ending reveals that you will experience numerous love affairs.

If the line of heart shows breaks under the ring of Saturn or near the line of Apollo, a broken engagement is indicated.

Unstable emotions are revealed if the line of heart is lightly chained.

If white spots appear on or near the line of heart, you will have an extremely happy love life.

A line which descends from the line of heart to the line of head denotes a broken engagement.

A line which ascends from the line of heart to the ring of Saturn is an indication of unrequited affections.

A line which runs from the line of heart to the line of Apollo reveals a troubled married life due to job or career interference.

The number of marriage lines found on your hand indicates the number of times you will be married in your life.

A straight line of marriage denotes a happy and contented married life.

However, an unhappy marriage filled with anger and sorrow is denoted if the line of marriage cuts through the line of Apollo.

If the line of marriage slopes down, you will outlive your spouse; but if it curves upward, it means that you will never marry.

Broken lines of marriage that overlap indicate periods of separation and reconciliation.

If a star or an island appears on the line of marriage, unfaithfulness is revealed.

You should not marry if your line of marriage is covered by many islands.

If the longest line of marriage is nearest to the pinky finger, you will marry in your later years; however, if it is closest to the line of heart, you will marry or enter into a love affair at a very young age.

An absent line of marriage means that marriage will not change the lives of either spouse.

A line running from the line of Saturn to the finger of Jupiter denotes a marriage blessed with love and happiness.

If the line of Apollo ends at the line of heart, you will marry a wealthy person or one who will become wealthy later on in life.

A tiny line that runs from the line of Apollo to the line of heart denotes a happy married life; however, if the line crosses over the line of heart, there will be a broken love affair.

A line of head that ends on the heart line reveals a person who makes great sacrifices for his or her lover.

A broken off fragmentary girdle of Venus indicates a disappointment in love.

Branched lines that descend from the line of life toward the thumb indicate that you are a person who possesses a strong desire for love and romance.

A triangle on the wrist indicates that you will marry a wealthy person.

A triangle that appears on or near the line of heart indicates a strong and happy marriage.

A cross on the mount of Jupiter means that you will have a happy married life, but you will also experience struggles.

A cross on the mount of Venus indicates that you will experience disappointment in love; while a star on the mount of Venus reveals that you are a happy person filled with great love for others.

9

Goddesses of Love

Throughout the history of mankind, nearly every pantheon contained at least one deity who personified the power of love and/or presided over marriage.

Although it would be next to impossible to include in the next two chapters the love deities worshipped in every culture since the dawn of time, all efforts have been made to list the names and descriptions of every major goddess and god associated with love and/or marriage, as well as many of the lesser-known love deities.

ALPAN, also known as Alpanu or Alpnu, is the Etruscan goddess of the art of love, as well as a goddess of the Underworld. In works of art, she is depicted as a winged woman wearing a cloak, sandals, and jewels.

APHRODITE is the ancient Greek goddess of love and beauty, and a deity who presided over human love, marriage ceremonies, and married life. She is depicted in art as a golden-haired, blue-eyed woman with pale skin and a beautiful face. She was also said to be notoriously unfaithful to her husband and lovers.

In Rome, she was identified with the goddess Venus, and in Greco- Roman Egypt, she was identified with and partially supplanted the goddess Hathor. Aphrodite was also identified with the lunar goddess Eurynome whose statue at Phigalia in Arcadia was a mermaid carved in wood.

The Greek love-goddess was also known by many different names including: Adonaia, Adonias, Cytherea, Mandragoris, and Aphrodite Anadyomene ("she who came out of the sea").

Among her children were Aeneas, Eros, Hymen, Harmonia, Priapus, and Hermaphroditus, who was half man and half woman.

In Homer's epic poem, *The Iliad*, Aphrodite is said to be the daughter of Zeus and his consort Dione, and through her mother was associated with the ancient worship at Dodona. However, in later legends, Aphrodite is described as the offspring of Uranos, coming forth from the foam of the sea and arriving in her scallop-shell at the myrtle grove in Cypress.

In Greek mythology, she was one of the Twelve Great Olympians, and the rival of the goddess Persephone for the love of the handsome Greek youth Adonis.

Aphrodite, whose name means "risen from sea foam," was identified in early Greek religious beliefs with the

Phoenician goddess Astarte and was known as Aphrodite Urania (Queen of the Heavens and personification of the power of love which unites heaven, earth, and the oceans into one harmonious system). She was also known as Aphrodite Pandemos, the personification of universal passion and earthly, or sensual, love. In later Greek literature, under Plato's influence, Aphrodite Urania was worshipped as the goddess of spiritual love. According to Homer, the Graces (Aglaia, Euphrosyne and Thalia) were the three Triple Goddess aspects of Aphrodite in triad.

The cult of Aphrodite was universal in the Mediterranean lands, and Aphrodisia (festivals in her honor) were celebrated frequently at her temples near the sea.

Her sacred colors are white, green, blue, and scarlet. Her sacred love- drawing gemstone is lapis lazuli; her metal is copper; and the trees sacred to her are the myrtle, myrrh, and palm. The aphrodisiacs sacred to Aphrodite and used by the Greeks were the tunny, sturgeon, scallop, periwinkle, and mandrake.

Aphrodite (and her Roman counterpart Venus) are the Neo-Pagan goddesses most invoked by Witches for the casting of love spells and rituals involving the making of aphrodisiacs, philtres and love charms, etc.

On May 6, 1938, the Long Island Church of Aphrodite was established in West Hempstead, New York, by the Reverend Gleb Botkin, a Russian author and son of the court physician to the last Czar of Russia.

ASERA is the love-goddess of the Semitic Amorites; identified with the Phoenician goddess Astarte. In the Ras Shamra texts she is described as the consort of El, the supreme god, and is known as the "mother of the gods."

ASTARTE is the ancient Phoenician goddess of love and fruitfulness, and the supreme female divinity of the Phoenician nations. She symbolizes all aspects of the female principle, as her male counterpart, Baal, symbolizes the male principle.

Astarte was worshipped at Tyre and Sidon, and was identified with various lunar and fertility deities, the Greek love-goddess Aphrodite, the Babylonian Ishtar, and the androgynous Baalith. The Israelites worshipped her after the conquest of Canaan, and her cult was also adopted by the Philistines.

In Phoenician art, Astarte is depicted as a woman robed in flames, armed with a bow and sword, and wearing the horns of a cow upon her head to symbolize her powers of fertility. (Because her horns are crescent-shaped, she is often mistakenly identified as a lunar goddess.) Sometimes she is depicted with a serpent or a child.

Since she was a fertility goddess, fruits of the season, newborn animals, and firstborn children were sacrificed to Astarte in primitive times in order to increase fertility in women, animals, and the earth.

Animals sacred to her are the gazelle, the cat, and the dove. Her sacred tree is the myrtle.

ASTHORETH is a horned love-goddess who was worshipped in the Palestine area. She is identified with Astarte.

BELILI is a Sumerian deity who preceded Ishtar as the beautiful goddess of love. She is also a lunar goddess, a goddess of trees, wells, and springs, and the ruler of the Underworld.

Belili, who is also known as Queen Belili, is both the sister and lover of the pomegranate-god Du'uzu, and from her name the familiar Biblical expression "Sons of Belial" derives. Her divinatory son Beli (identified with the Babylonian Earth-god Bel) was originally the god of willow trees, and later became the Great God of Light.

CERES is the old Italic goddess of marriage and of fertility. Her sacred feast, the Cerealia, was celebrated on the nineteenth of April.

CREIRWY is the Celtic goddess of love and beauty, and the daughter of the poetry goddess Keridwen. According to Celtic mythology, Creirwy was the most beautiful woman in the world, and her brother Avaggdu was the ugliest man.

ERATO is the muse of love poetry and marriage songs. In ancient Greek art, she appears wearing a wreath of myrtle and roses (sacred to the love goddess Venus), and playing on a large lyre with many strings.

ERZULIE is the Rada Voodoo goddess (or loa) of love, beauty, and femininity. Her primary attribute is luxury, and she is envisaged as a young, beautiful, wealthy lady wearing many golden rings and necklaces. Her favorite drink is champagne and, like the Virgin Mary, her symbol is a pierced heart. But unlike the Virgin Mary, Erzulie possesses a highly erotic character. She is the consort of both Ogoun, the god of fire and war, and Agwe, the royal god of the sea.

In her Petro form, she is known as Erzulie Ge-Rouge (Erzulie Red Eyes) and is envisaged as a pale, trembling woman who sobs uncontrollably because no one can love her enough.

White and pink are her colors, and she is worshipped on Friday—her sacred day of the week.

ESMERALDA is a South American goddess of love and beauty. Emerald green is her sacred color, and emerald is the love-drawing gemstone dedicated to her.

FREYA is the Norse goddess of love, beauty, and the art of healing. In Norse mythology, she is the consort of the sunshine-god Odur, the daughter of Njord and Skald, and the sister of Frey (the lord of peace and prosperity). She is also known as Freia, Fri, Fria, or Freyja, and in Germany she was identified with the goddess Frigga.

In works of art, Freya is depicted as a voluptuous woman with golden hair and blue eyes, riding across the sky in a golden chariot drawn by white cats. According to mythology, she possessed a falcon garb which gave her the power to fly, and a magickal necklace of amber beads fashioned by the four dwarfs in Svartalfaheim and known as Brisingamen.

Amber is the gemstone dedicated to Freya. Friday is her sacred day, and cats were her symbols and familiars.

A sisterhood of priestess-seers known as the Volva evolved around the worship of Freya. The Volva knew the secrets of magickal transformation and were famous for their accurate prophecies and abilities to change themselves into cats and other animals.

FRIGGA is another Norse goddess of love, and the patroness of marriage and fecundity. (In Teutonic mythology, she is known as Fricka.) Through her eleven handmaidens, she reunites parted lovers and presides over married love. Keys are her symbols and rams are the animals sacred to her.

In works of art, she is depicted as a beautiful and naked Lady Godiva-like woman with flowing golden hair, wearing a torque and bracelets on her arms and legs. Sometimes she appears as a tall, stately woman in long robes of ivory white with keys hanging from her girdle.

HATHOR is the ancient Egyptian goddess of love, beauty, and mirth, the patroness of women, infants, music, and marriage, and the female principle. At her sanctuary at Dendera, she was also worshipped as both a lunar goddess and a fertility goddess.

As a mother-goddess and cosmic deity, she was identified principally with the goddess Isis and other earlier Egyptian goddesses. As a sky-goddess, she was the "Queen of Heaven," the Creatrix, and the Great Mother, identified with the Babylonian Ishtar and the Phoenician Astarte.

In works of art, Hathor is depicted as either a cow or as a woman with the head of a cow, wearing between her crescent-shaped horns the headdress of two plumes and a solar disc decorated with stars to symbolize her role as a sky-goddess and creatrix.

HERA was the Greek guardian of wedlock, whose Roman counterpart was Juno. Her symbols are the peacock, the diadem, and the scepter. The animal sacred to her is the cow.

INANNA is the ancient Sumerian goddess of both love and war, mother- goddess, and "Queen of Heaven," later identified with the Babylonian love- and-war goddess Ishtar. Her symbol is the reed-bundle, and her descent to the Underworld is the subject of a famous Sumerian poem.

ISHTAR, who was worshipped by the Phoenicians under the name of Astarte, is the Assyrian, Babylonian, and Neo-Pagan goddess of love and fertility. She personified the planet Venus, and was identified with the Sumerian goddess Inanna and the Biblical Ashtoreth.

Ishtar is one of the great figures in Babylonian mythology, and is a deity with two principal aspects: In her first aspect as a goddess of love and fertility, she is compassionate, gentle, and loving. In her second aspect as a war-goddess, she is cruel, aggressive, and lustful. (It was said that in her second aspect, she was so terrible that she made even the gods tremble while warriors sang her praise.)

The lion was the cult animal of Ishtar; the Tree of Life

was her symbol; and her womb was believed to be the never-ending source of the water of life.

KADES is the ancient Canaanite goddess of love, beauty, and sexuality. In works of art, she is depicted as a beautiful naked woman riding a lion and holding a serpent in her hands.

KUBABA is the ancient love-goddess and mother-goddess of Asia Minor, worshipped in Upper Mesopotamia as Gubaba. She is identified with the Hurrian love-goddess Sauska. The mirror and the pomegranate are sacred to her.

MELUSINE is a love-goddess who appeared as a beautiful woman with the tail of a fish. She was worshipped by the followers of the medieval Love cults in southern France.

MINNE was a Pagan goddess who granted women and men permission to engage in lovemaking. Her name was a synonym for "love," and she was often called Lofn ("Goddess Love"). In medieval times, Minne (like Melusine) was worshipped as a mermaid-tailed Aphrodite by Minne-singers and Minstrels.

NANAJA is the ancient Mesopotamian goddess of love and sexuality, whose cult spread to Syria and Persia during the Hellenistic period. Like Ishtar, she was also a goddess of both love and war.

ODUDUA is a love-goddess of the Yoruba people in Nigeria. She is also an earth-goddess and a deity associated with Vodoun fertility cults. Her sacred and magickal color is black.

The love-goddess *OLWEN* is known as both the "Laughing Aphrodite of Welsh Legend" and "She of the White

Track." She is depicted in ancient works of art as a beautiful woman with yellow hair and pale skin, and it is said that white trefoils spring up wherever she treads to symbolize her Summer aspect of the old Triple Goddess.

OSHUN is an orisha (deity) of the Afro-Cuban religion of Santeria. She is a beautiful river goddess and the patroness of love, marriage, and fertility. She is essentially the archetype of joy and pleasure, and the lover of many deities, including Chango—the master of thunder, lightning, and fire who symbolizes passion and desire.

Oshun rules the abdominal region and the sexual organs of the human body. Her sacred number is five; her sacred colors are yellow and white; and her Feast Day is September 8. The pumpkin is sacred to her (as are seashells, honey, and mirrors), and many of her love spells and rituals call for the use of pumpkins. Her sacred symbols are fans, mirrors, and boats.

PATTINI is an ancient marriage-goddess who was worshipped by the Singhalese of Ceylon. According to myth, she was born from a mango which had been struck by a divine arrow.

PRENDE is an ancient Illyrian love-goddess who was the consort of the thunder-god Perendi. Like Venus and many other goddesses of love, her sacred day of the week is Friday.

SAPPHO was a famous Lesbian poet/priestess of Seventh Century Greece, recently deified by many Lesbian-oriented Witch covens as the Neo- Pagan "goddess" of Lesbian love and the patroness of gay women and female poets. She was born on the island of Lesbos (a sacred colony known as the "Isle of Women") and was dedicated to the worship of the female principle.

As a poetess, she was known for her beautiful lyric poetry, and was once called the Tenth Muse. She wrote nine
books of odes, elegies, and hymns, including Ode to
Aphrodite. She also invented the verse form known as Sap-
phics.

Unfortunately, because of her sexual preference for
other women and devotion to a Pagan goddess, later writ-
ers of antiquity accused Sappho of vice and immorality,
and few of her works were able to escape the book burn-
ings of the early era of closed-minded Christianity.

She was once married, but devoted her later life to the
love of women. However, the story of Sappho commonly
alluded to is that she took her own life by leaping from the
promontory of Leucadia because of unrequited love for the
beautiful youth known as Phaon.

SAUSKA (also known as Sawuska or Sausga) is a
winged goddess of love and beauty. She was worshipped
by the ancient Hurrians of Asia Minor, and identified with
the goddess Ishtar. The lion is the animal sacred to her.

TURAN, a winged love-goddess identified with Aphrodite and Venus, was worshipped by the Etruscans in
Northern Italy during the years 900–500 B.C. Her attributes
are a dove and a swan, often accompanied by a twig or a
flower blossom.

VENUS is the ancient Roman goddess of love and
beauty, the personification of sexuality, fertility, prosperity, and good luck, and the counterpart of the Greek love-
goddess Aphrodite. Venus is also identified with Astarte,
Inanna, and Ishtar, and linked to the Jewish Kabbalah as
one of the seven celestial hierarchies—the angel of love
known as Anael.

In mythology, Venus was the daughter of Jupiter and

Dione, the unfaithful wife of Vulcan, and the lover of many gods and mortals, including Mars, Anchises, and the handsome shepherd youth known as Adonis. In other legends, Venus (like her Greek counterpart Aphrodite) was said to have been born from the foam of the sea. The west wind wafted her gently along the ocean waves to the isle of Cyprus, where she was received and attired by the Seasons, and then led to the assembly of the gods who were all charmed by her beautiful features.

In imperial times, she was worshipped under several aspects. As Venus Genetrix, she was worshipped as the mother of the Roman race and the Trojan hero Aeneaes; as Venus Felix, the goddess of good fortune; as Venus Verticordia, the protectress of feminine chastity; and as Venus Victrix, the goddess of victory.

Venus possessed a magickal embroidered girdle called Cestus which made its wearer, male or female, the object of passionate love and desire.

The month of April was held sacred to her because of its association with Spring as the season of love; and her festival, known as the Veneralia, was celebrated in her honor each year in Roman gardens. The festival consisted of nocturnal dances and passionate pleasures.

The symbols of Venus were the white swan, the dove, dolphin, hare, ram, and tortoise. The plants sacred to her were the rose and the myrtle tree, of which she was especially fond; hence she was known as Venus Myrtea.

In addition to Venus, the Romans of ancient times also worshipped other lesser-known goddesses who were associated with love: THALASSA, an archaic form of Aphrodite Marina, was the patroness of sex and marriage. She was invoked at weddings by the holy wedding cry of "Talassio!" JUNO was another patroness of marriage. Her sacred month was June (the traditional wedding month) and her sacred symbols were the peacock, the cowrie shell, and the lily. *SALACIA* was the goddess of weddings; and *FEBRUA* was the goddess of erotic love.

VOR is the ancient Germanic guardian of marriage whose name means "she who is cautious." Oaths and pledges are sacred to her.

XOCHIQUETZAL is the ancient Aztec goddess of love, beauty, and flowers, consort of the Mexican sun-god, Moon-Virgin, and Fairy Queen. Her sacred flower is the marigold, and like many of the ancient Indo-European love-goddesses, her sacred symbol is the white dove. She presided over the twentieth day of the Aztec calendar, and, according to mythology, lived high on a mountaintop surrounded by musicians and dancers. Her name means "upright flower."

Other deities worshipped as goddesses of love include the Pagan goddess *HABONDIA* (who is also known as the "Lady of Love"); *KIVAN-NON* (the Japanese equivalent of the Roman love-goddess Venus); the Polish *DZYDZILELYA*; and *TLAZOLTEOTL*, who was known as the "Mother of All Gods," and worshipped in Mexico as well as in Central America.

10

Gods of Love

AIRYAMAN is the ancient Aryan god of marriage. He is identified with *ARYAMAN*, the Vedic patron of marriage who appears in the Rigveda as the founder of matrimony.

AIZEN MYO-O is the Japanese god of love and beauty who represents loving passion transformed into the desire for illumination. In Oriental art, he is depicted as having three eyes and six arms, each holding different attributes. His ferocious-looking face is crowned by the head of a lion with a bristling mane surmounted by a thunderbolt which calms evil passions and guilty desires. His name means "love" and he is filled with compassion for mankind despite his terrifying appearance.

ANGUS is the Celtic god of love and beauty, the patron of youths and maidens, and a deity often called the Irish Adonis. He was also known as Angus Og (or Oc), Angus the Young, or Angus of the Brug. His name means "son of the young" and he was known for his beautiful golden hair and physical beauty.

On his harp of gold, he played sweet, romantic melodies, and his kisses turned into bright birds which hovered protectingly over the heads of young lovers.

In old Irish mythology, he was the son of the Earth-god Dagda ("the good god") and Boann, the Queen of the Side (the divine race of Ireland.)

One Celtic myth tells how Angus gave a mantle of invisibility to the lovers Diarmait and Grainne to enable them to escape from the clutches of Finn, the leader of a band of warriors (the Fenians) who, in his old age, desired to marry the beautiful maiden Grainne himself.

BES is the ancient Egyptian marriage-god who appears in the form of a bearded dwarf wearing a headdress of ostrich feathers. He is also the patron of dance, music, and mirth; the protector of expectant mothers and children; and the guardian of sleep who chases away bad spirits and sends the sleeper sweet dreams.

Bes was one of the most popular gods in Egypt, and his image was a talisman against evil omen and sorcery which appeared in Egyptian homes more than that of any other deity.

BHAGA is the Vedic god of marriage, to whom the month of Spring is dedicated.

CUPID, also known as Amor, is the mischievous god of erotic love in Roman mythology. He is identified with the Greek god Eros, and is depicted as a winged infant with a chubby face. However, before 300 B.C., Cupid was originally portrayed as a handsome, athletic youth.

Cupid was the son and constant companion of the love-goddess Venus. He was armed with a magickal bow and arrow, and shot the "darts of love" into the bosoms of both gods and mortals.

In classical mythology, Cupid was united with the beautiful mortal Psyche after his mother's intense jealousy was overcome. Psyche became the personification of a soul filled with the passion of love, and was represented in works of art as a beautiful maiden with the wings of a butterfly.

EROS is the Greek god of erotic love, and the son of Aphrodite and Zeus. He was represented in early mythology as one of the primeval forces of Nature, the son of Chaos, and the embodiment of the harmony and creative power in the universe. In later mythology, he became the constant attendant of his mother, the love-goddess Aphrodite. Plato said that Eros was the "oldest of gods," and according to the Orphics, he was the first deity to emerge from the womb of Mother Night, the primal creatress.

In Greek works of art, Eros was represented as a handsome, winged youth with fair skin and hair of golden curls. His eyes are often covered with a blindfold to symbolize the blindness of love.

Eros was identified with the Hindu love-god Kama, and like his Roman counterpart Cupid, he would fire golden arrows from his bow, bringing love to those whose bosoms they would strike. His sacred festival, the Erotidia, was celebrated in ancient Greece, and he was worshipped at Thespiae in Boeotia and at Parion in Mysia.

HYACINTHUS is a Spring flower-god who was worshipped in ancient Crete, Mycenae, Rhodes, and Sparta. He is deified by many gay male Witches as the Neo-Pagan deity or patron of gay love.

The hyacinth is the flower sacred to him (and named after him), and in Lacedaemon, his flowers were symbolic of the phallus.

In classical mythology, Hyacinthus was a beautiful youth who was accidentally killed by the discus of his homosexual lover, the Greek sun-god Apollo. In another story, Zephyr, the West Wind, was also in love with the fair Hyacinthus, and in his jealous anger at seeing Apollo preferred to him, he blew his mighty breath upon the sun-god's discus and caused it to strike the forehead of Hyacinthus, killing him instantly. As the weeping Apollo held the lifeless body of his lover to his breast, Hyacinthus's blood dripped onto the ground, causing a wonderful lily-shaped flower of deep purple to blossom. Apollo inscribed the petals with Hyacinthus's initial as a memorial of the great god's sorrow.

HYMEN (also known as Hymenaeus) is a deity who was worshipped by both the Greeks and the Romans as the god of marriage and wedding feasts, the founder and protector of marriage rights, and the personification of the marriage song. In ancient Greece, he was invoked as part of every marriage celebration. He was the attendant of the love-goddess Aphrodite, whose son he was by Dionysus, the Greek god of vegetation, fertility, and wine. At other times, he is said to have been born a mortal and later deified.

In works of art, Hymen is represented as a beautiful youth with golden hair and the soft, delicate face of a girl. He carries a wedding torch and a garland, or a veil. Sometimes he appears nude, and often he is winged.

According to mythology, Hymen was a young man who

died on his wedding day when the house caved in on top of him, and thus he was invoked to appease his spirit. In another story, Hymen is said to have saved a group of women from evil pirates. For his heroic deed, he was rewarded by having marriage songs named for him.

In the Orphic belief, Hymen was brought back from the dead by Aesculapius, the Roman god of medicine and healing.

KAMA (also known as Kamadeva) is the Hindu god of love, and the personification of desire. He rules both men and gods, and is endowed with the gift of eternal youth. He is the son of Vishnu and Lakshmi; however, in various texts he is said to be the offspring of Dharma and Sraddha, a deity born from water, and even the product of Brahma's urgic meditation. His name means literally "desire," and he is identified with the love-gods Cupid and Eros.

In works of art, Kama is depicted as an excessively handsome youth riding on the back of an elephant, a giant parrot, or a dove. He carries a sugarcane bow with a bowstring of bees and arrows tipped with flowers. He is symbolized by a piscine monster, often shown in a red banner.

The Hindu myth associated with Kama tells how he stole into the garden of Siva and attempted to pierce the god's heart with one of his flower-tipped arrows of love. Kama took aim and fired, but before the shaft could reach its target, a powerful bolt of fire shot from Siva's great third eye and Kama was burned to ashes.

MENU is the Egyptian equivalent of the Greek god Eros.

SVAROG is the Slavonic god of both fire and the sun, who was regarded at one time as the founder of matrimony.

TUTUNIS was the phallic god of Roman weddings.

XOCHIPILLI is the Aztec god of love, marriage, flowers, music, and youth. He is the consort of the goddess Xochiquetzal, and the main character of an ancient Vernal Equinox fertility rite.

11

Handfasting

Handfasting (sometimes known as handfesting) is an old Wiccan betrothal ceremony in which the hands of the bride and groom are tied together with a consecrated knotted cord to signify that they have been joined together in matrimonial union. The rite is usually performed by either the High Priestess or High Priest of the coven (if the wedding is nonlegal) or by a legally recognized minister if a legally binding wedding is preferred. (Before being legally wed, many Wiccan couples prefer to live in a common-law

162 Wicca Love Spells

"trial" marriage which can be dissolved by the High Priestess at the end of the year if either the husband or the wife is dissatisfied with the arrangement.)

The Pagan tradition of "Jumping the Broom," in which the bride and groom both jump over a broomstick, is an ancient form of a common-law marriage ceremony practiced in certain parts of Scotland, Denmark, and China, and quite popular among the Gypsies. The Broom Jump is performed at the end of the Handfasting Rite.

Wiccan Handfasting Ceremony

The following wedding ceremony is a non-legally binding spiritual commitment rite which can be performed by either the coven's High Priestess or High Priest.

Before the ceremony is carried out, it is extremely important that the entire area where the handfasting is to take place be consecrated by salt, water, and any purifying incense such as cedar, frankincense, sage, or sandalwood.

Erect the altar and place upon it everything needed for the ceremony: two white candles, a censer of incense, a dish of salt or soil, a brass altar bell, a wand, a chalice of water, a cup of rose oil for anointing, a quartz crystal, the wedding rings, and two white cords. Next to the altar, place a large straw broom to be used in the traditional Broom Jump at the end of the rite.

Cast a circle in a clockwise direction, using an athame or ceremonial sword, and after each guest has been blessed with greetings and incense, ring the altar bell to signal the start of the ceremony.

The bride and groom should enter the circle, holding hands. Bless them with incense and greetings, and then have them stand facing you and the altar (North) as the wedding guests gather around the perimeter of the circle, joining all hands together to form a human chain. Facing the bride and groom, raise your arms up to the sky and say:

IN THIS SACRED CIRCLE OF LIGHT
WE GATHER IN PERFECT LOVE
AND PERFECT TRUST.
O GODDESS OF DIVINE LOVE
I ASK THEE TO BLESS THIS COUPLE,
THEIR LOVE, AND THEIR MARRIAGE
FOR AS LONG AS THEY SHALL LIVE

IN LOVE TOGETHER.
MAY THEY EACH ENJOY A HEALTHY LIFE
FILLED WITH JOY, LOVE, STABILITY,
AND FERTILITY.

Hold the dish of salt or soil before them and let each of them place their right hand over the dish as you say:

BLESSED BE
BY THE ANCIENT AND MYSTICAL
ELEMENT OF EARTH.
MAY THE GODDESS OF LOVE
IN ALL OF HER GLORY
BLESS YOU WITH LOVE, TENDERNESS,
HAPPINESS, AND COMPASSION
FOR AS LONG AS YE BOTH SHALL LIVE.

Return the dish of salt or soil to the altar. The couple should now turn and face East. Ring the altar bell thrice and then smudge the couple with incense, and say:

BLESSED BE BY SMOKE AND BELL,
SYMBOLS OF THE ANCIENT AND MYSTICAL
ELEMENT OF AIR.
MAY THE GODDESS OF LOVE
IN ALL OF HER GLORY
BLESS YOU WITH COMMUNICATION,
INTELLECTUAL GROWTH, AND WISDOM
FOR AS LONG AS YE BOTH SHALL LIVE.

Return the censer of incense to the altar. The couple should now turn and face South. Hand each of them a white candle to hold in their right hand. Light the candles, and then take the wand from the altar and hold it above them as you say:

BLESSED BE BY WAND AND FLAME,
SYMBOLS OF THE ANCIENT AND MYSTICAL
ELEMENT OF FIRE.
MAY THE GODDESS OF LOVE
IN ALL OF HER GLORY
BLESS YOU WITH HARMONY, VITALITY,
CREATIVITY, AND PASSION
FOR AS LONG AS YE BOTH SHALL LIVE.

Return the candles and wand to the altar. The couple
should now turn and face West. Take the chalice of water
and sprinkle some of the water over their heads as you
say:

BLESSED BE
BY THE ANCIENT AND MYSTICAL
ELEMENT OF WATER.
MAY THE GODDESS OF LOVE
IN ALL OF HER GLORY
BLESS YOU WITH FRIENDSHIP, INTUITION,
CARING, AND UNDERSTANDING
FOR AS LONG AS YE BOTH SHALL LIVE.

Return the chalice of water to the altar. The couple
should once again turn and face North. Anoint their fore-
heads with rose oil, and then hold the quartz crystal over
them as a sacred symbol of the spiritual realm as you say:

MAY THE DIVINE GODDESS OF LOVE
IN ALL OF HER GLORY
BLESS YE WITH TOGETHERNESS,
HONESTY, AND SPIRITUAL GROWTH
FOR AS LONG AS YE BOTH SHALL LIVE.
MAY THE GOD AND GODDESS WITHIN YE

GUIDE YE ON THE RIGHT PATH
AND MAY THE MAGICK OF YOUR LOVE
CONTINUE TO GROW FOR AS LONG
AS YE REMAIN TOGETHER IN LOVE,
FOR YOUR MARRIAGE IS A SACRED UNION
OF THE FEMALE AND MALE ASPECTS
OF DIVINITY.

Return the crystal to the altar, and consecrate the wedding rings with a sprinkle of salt and water as you say:

BY SALT AND WATER
I PURIFY AND CLEANSE
THESE BEAUTIFUL SYMBOLS OF LOVE.
LET ALL NEGATIVE VIBRATIONS,
IMPURITIES, AND HINDRANCES
BE CAST FORTH HENCEFROM!
AND LET ALL THAT IS POSITIVE,
LOVING, AND GOOD
ENTER HEREIN.
BLESSED BE THESE RINGS
IN THE DIVINE NAME OF THE GODDESS.
SO MOTE IT BE.

The groom now places the bride's ring upon her finger, and she in turn places the other one on his. They may now exchange their vows which each has written in their own words prior to the ceremony.

After the couple's vows of love have been spoken, consecrate the cords in the same manner as the wedding rings, and then, holding the cords side by side, have the man and woman each take an end and tie a knot as they express their love to each other. Tie a knot in the middle of the cord and say:

BY THE KNOTS ON THIS CORD
YOUR LOVE IS UNITED.

Take the knotted cord and tie together the hands of the
bride and her groom. Visualize a white light of Goddess
energy and protection surround the couple as their auras
join together as one, and everyone attending the ceremony
raises energy by repeatedly and joyously chanting: LOVE!
LOVE! LOVE!

After you have projected the power raised into the bride
and groom and their marriage, allow for a few moments of
silence, and then remove the cord from their hands and
say:

BY THE POWER OF THE GODDESS
AND HER HORNED CONSORT
I NOW PRONOUNCE YE
HUSBAND AND WIFE
FOR AS LONG AS YE BOTH
SHALL LIVE TOGETHER IN LOVE.
SO MOTE IT BE.

The guests may now cheer, applaud, and congratulate
the newlywed couple. Give thanks to the Goddess and
God, and then uncast the circle. Lay the straw broom horizontally on the ground and have the bride and groom leap
over it together as they hold onto each other's hands.

The Wiccan Handfasting Rite is now ended, and should
be celebrated by all with wine and cake.

12

Love Divination

The magickal and mystical art of love divination is a practice of the greatest antiquity, and countless means have been used in the past, and are still used today, for this purpose.

Love divination is a form of sympathetic magick. Its practice (past and present) is universal, and it has always been a vital part of the Old Religion.

It was widely practiced by temple magicians of ancient

Egypt, the augurs of Rome, Mexico, and Peru, and many of the Indian tribes of North America.

Many twentieth century customs are rooted in the ancient practice of love divination. For instance, the relatively modern Halloween custom of bobbing for apples is actually a remnant of ancient Druidic divination.

The daisy (the symbol of fidelity) is used in what is perhaps the most popular and well-known form of love divination, commonly practiced by children and young teens in England and the United States. To determine whether or not the love of your boyfriend (or girlfriend) is true, pluck the petals from a daisy while repeating the famous words "He loves me. He loves me not."

The daisy is also used in another method of love divination to determine how many years will pass before you get married. Pluck a handful of grass and daisies with your eyes closed, and the number of daisies that you find in the bunch will indicate the number of years.

To test the faithfulness of your lover, place a poppy petal on top of your left fist and then strike it with your right hand. If it makes a popping sound, it is a sign that your lover is true. If not, your lover has not been a faithful one.

Place two laurel leaves under your pillow on St. Valentine's Day to enable you to dream of your future lover.

To find out the initial of your future lover's name, peel an apple in one long, continuous strip and then toss the peel over your left shoulder. Whichever letter of the alphabet it forms will be the initial.

Twist the stem of an apple as you recite the letters of the alphabet and whichever letter you are on when the stem comes off will be the initial of your future lover's name. (If you reach the end of the alphabet, begin again at the letter A.)

A borrowed wedding ring suspended over a glass of water from a south- running stream by a hair from the head of an unmarried woman will determine whether or not she will ever marry. If the ring turns around quickly, it is a prediction of marriage; two marriages if it revolves slowly; and spinsterhood if it hits the rim of the glass.

If an unmarried girl counts the number of cuckoo's notes first heard in the Spring, she will know how many years will pass before she is married.

To determine the character of a future wife, according to a Colonial American folk method of divination, a young man must find out his beloved's age and then seek the appropriate corresponding verse from the first chapter of the Book of Proverbs.

To see the image of future husbands, medieval maidens would stand in front of a mirror with an apple, slice it into nine pieces, impale each piece on the point of a knife, holding it over their left shoulders.

To predict a happy marriage, young men in the Orient pick a bachelor's button (cornflower) at dawn and carry it in their pocket for twenty-four hours. If the flower stays fresh, the marriage will be good; if the flower withers, me young man will soon find a new love.

According to an old folk custom in Austria, if an apple cut on Saint Thomas' Eve (December 20) contains an even number of seeds, it indicates a wedding. If one of the seeds is cut in half, it foretells a troubled marriage. If two seeds are cut, it is an omen of widowhood.

To test the fidelity of a lover, according to a rural American custom, light a candle outdoors near his or her house. If the flame burns toward you or your lover's house, your lover is faithful. If not, your lover is faithless.

On a night of the full moon, place under your pillow the Major Arcana card of the Tarot deck known as "The Lovers" to induce prophetic dreams about your future lover as you sleep.

To make bachelors see their future brides in a dream, according to a medieval treatise on oneiromancy (dream interpretation), mix together magnate dust and powdered coral with the blood of a white pigeon to form a dough. En-close it in a large fig, wrap it in a piece of blue cloth, and then wear it around your neck when you go to sleep.

To dream of your future husband, sleep with a petticoat, garter, daisy roots, an onion, or a piece of wedding cake under your head. Tie a poplar branch to your stockings or socks and place them under your pillow, or rub your tem-ples with a few drops of dove's blood before going to sleep.

If you cannot decide between several lovers, scratch the name of each man or woman on a separate onion. Leave the onions in a warm place and the one that sprouts first will denote the more passionate love.

To see the face of your future spouse, look through smoked glass into an unused well on May Day, pick twelve sage leaves as the clock strikes noon on Saint Mark's Day, or walk downstairs backward on Halloween night holding a lighted candle over your head and then turn around sud-denly upon reaching the last step.

Other Halloween night love divinations: To see a shadow of your future wife, crawl underneath a black-berry bush. To make the image of your future husband ap-pear before you, run three times around your house with a willow branch in your right hand, saying: "He that is going to be my husband, come and grip." To find out the initials of a future love-mate, catch a snail and keep it in a covered dish all night while you sleep. In the morning, the initials will be formed by the snail's trail of slime. To find out who your future husband will be, take a bunch of apples and write the name of a potential suitor on each one. Place the apples over a blazing fire, and the person whose name on the apple which pops first will be the one you will marry.

To find out who will be your future spouse, write the names of several potential suitors on small slips of paper on Saint Valentine's Day. Stick each slip into a ball of clay and drop them into a container of water; the ball of clay that rises to the surface first will contain the name of your true love.

Write the name of your lover on a nut and place it upon a live coal. If it jumps, it is a sign that your lover has been unfaithful to you. However, if the nut burns and blazes, it indicates that your lover is true.

An old Irish method of love divination is to gather ten ivy leaves in silence on Halloween night. Throw away one of the leaves and place the remaining ones under your pillow before you go to bed. You will then dream of your future marriage mate.

To find out from which direction your lover will come, hold a ladybug on your fingertip and tell it to "Fly away home." The direction that the ladybug flies will be the one.

To spell out the name of your future husband or wife, perform the following method of love divination on Halloween night: Tie a wedding ring to a silk thread and hold it suspended within a goblet. Recite the letters of the alphabet and whenever the ring strikes the side of the goblet, write down the letter and then begin reciting the alphabet again. Repeat until the name of your future love partner has been spelled out, possibly in a scrambled form.

Pour some melted wax through a wedding ring into a container of water or white wine. If the wax cools in the shape of a bell, it indicates a wedding.

To test the fidelity of your lover, kneel beside your bed and twine together two rose stems. If the color of the roses begin to appear darker, it is a sign that your lover has been faithful to you.

To see an image of your future spouse, make a "Witch's chain" of juniper and mistletoe berries tied with acorns and wound around a branch. Cast the chain into a blazing hearthfire and as the last acorn burns, a vision will come to you.

To dream of your future husband or wife, collect nine leaves of a "female" holly at the stroke of midnight on a

Friday. Place them in a three- cornered handkerchief tied with nine knots and place the charm under your pillow before going to sleep. (This charm is said to work only if no words are spoken until the following sunrise.)

Look into a looking glass on Saint Agnes' Eve to see the image of your future spouse.

To make your lover appear before you in a dream, pluck some wild yarrow from a graveyard and place it under your pillow at night before going to sleep.

To test the fidelity of your lover, give him (or her) a star sapphire as a love gift. If your lover has been untrue to you, the stone will turn pale.

To discover how many years will pass before you wed, according to old country lore of England, pick a dandelion and the number of puffs it takes for you to blow off all of its fuzzy seeds will indicate the number of years you must wait.

Hang your handkerchief on a bush on May Eve, and at dawn the initials of your future spouse will be formed in dew on the linen surface, according to country folk in the Ozark Mountains region.

To find out what your future husband's occupation will be, drop a bit of molten lead into a container of cool rainwater. The shape that the lead forms into will symbolize his job.

Love Numerology

1	2	3	4	5	6	7	8	9
A	B	C	D	E	F	G	H	I
J	K	L	M	N	O	P	Q	R
S	T	U	V	W	X	Y	Z	

For an ideal relationship, according to most numerologists, you and your love mate should share the same love number.

To find out what your love number is, simply add up the numerological values of your full name (using the chart above) with the date of your birth. Add three (the mystical number of magick) and then add together the digits of the total number if higher than nine until the number is reduced to a single- digit number. You now have your love number.

For example, the love number for John Doe, whose birthdate is June 14, 1951, is the number 2:

```
J O H N  D O E
1 6 8 5  4 6 5 Total: 35
                  +
Birthdate: 6-14-1951 Total: 27
                  +
Magick Number 3    Total:  3
                          ───
                           65  (6 + 5) = 11 (1 + 1) = 2
```

13

Love Omens

It is lucky to be kissed while standing under mistletoe; however, if the girl refuses to be kissed, she will remain a spinster.

Itchy lips are a sign that you will soon be kissed. If the right side of your body itches, it is a sign that a lover is thinking about you. An itchy nose indicates a secret admirer.

If a young unmarried girl loses her apron, it is a sign that her lover or future husband is thinking about her at that moment. An old German folk belief is that if a man wipes his hands on the apron of a girl, he will fall passionately in love with her. However, once they are engaged, if he should ever touch her apron while she wears it, they will have a marriage filled with quarrels.

According to an unusual German superstition, if a girl urinates into a man's shoe, he will fall madly in love with her.

An ash leaf placed inside the left shoe of a young girl will cause her to marry the first gentleman she encounters, according to an old English belief.

In Slavonia, it is believed that a woman can make a man fall in love with her by secretly making him eat the heart of a black cat killed at the new moon.

According to an old New England superstition, if a girl takes the last puff of a cigar or steps on a cigar end, she will fall in love with the first man she sees.

It is said that the seventh day after the full moon is the best time for a boy and girl to meet and fall in love at first sight.

If your shoelaces come undone, this is a sign that your true love is thinking about you.

If you sneeze on a Tuesday, you will kiss a stranger. If you sneeze on a Saturday, you will see your true love on the following day. If two lovers sneeze at the same time, it is an omen of good fortune.

If an unmarried girl turns a kettle so that the spout faces a wall or chimney, she will die a spinster.

Should an unmarried girl look through a keyhole on Saint Valentine's Day and see a cock and hen together, she will receive a marriage proposal before the end of the year.

It is an old belief that a ladybug will fly off in the direction from which a future spouse will come.

Eating ant eggs with honey was at one time believed to be an antidote for love sickness!

According to an old English superstition, should a man kill a glowworm, he and his love will soon part.

If two lovers share the same towel after swimming or bathing, they will soon part.

According to an old German folk belief, a hairpin that falls from a woman's hair is a sign that she will soon lose her love.

If you part from your lover beside a bridge, you will part forever.

To give your lover a handkerchief as a gift means that you will soon part and never marry, according to European folk belief.

A woman who lets her lover carry her comb will later lose his love to another woman.

A cobweb on a woman's door is an omen that her lover has been untrue.

A burning candle placed in a window will ensure the safe return of a lover, while a pink candle burned on Saint Valentine's Day will bring true love.

Ivy grows profusely on the graves of young maidens who have died of broken hearts.

To dream about broken eggs is an omen of a lover's quarrel.

Never cut parsley if you are in love, or else bad luck will come your way.

If you pick a pansy with the dew still on it, you will cause your lover's death.

According to folk belief, if the first bird a young woman sees on Saint Valentine's Day morning is a bluebird, her future lover will be a happy man. If she sees a crossbill, he will be argumentative. If she sees a robin, he will be a sailor. If she sees a blackbird, he will be a clergyman or a priest. If she sees a goldfinch or any other bird of a yellow color, he will be a wealthy man. If she sees a sparrow, he will be a farmer. If she sees a dove, he will be a peaceful man. However, if the first bird seen on Saint Valentine's day is a woodpecker, it is an omen that she will never wed.

It is unlucky for two lovers to drive behind a pair of white horses.

Love Letters

Love letters should always be written in ink and mailed on Fridays (which is the day of the week ruled by Venus, the goddess of love).

It is unlucky to mail love letters on February 29, September 1, Christmas Day, or any Sunday.

Setting fire to a love letter will bring an end to the love affair; however, according to an old folk belief, if you burn one of your lover's letters, the size and color of the flames will enable you to determine whether or not your lover has been faithful and true to you. If the flames burn high and light- colored, the love is strong; if the flames burn weak and blue, the love affair is doomed.

If your hand trembles while you write a love letter, it is a good sign that means your love is reciprocated. If the ink blots, it means that your loved one is thinking fond thoughts of you.

If a girl receives two love letters from two different men at the same time, it is an omen that neither man will be her future husband.

To receive a love letter that is insufficiently stamped is an omen that the love affair is coming to an end. The same applies to love letters that arrive damaged or with the flaps open.

Engagement

If a man proposes to a woman on Christmas Eve and she accepts, they will surely have a happy married life together; however, if he proposes to her in a church, the marriage will be cursed with bad luck.

According to an old folk belief, a young girl will receive a marriage proposal if she is unexpectedly kissed by a man with a dark complexion or if she kisses a man with a mustache and a hair from it sticks to her lips.

It is extremely unlucky for a man to propose to a woman (or vice versa) on a bus, train, plane, or in any public place.

To avoid bad luck and sorrow, an engaged woman should keep from touching her right hand with her left until her wedding day.

An engagement ring containing pearls is believed to bring unhappiness to the marriage.

An unhappy marriage is portended if a member of the parish passes away during the engagement period.

According to British folk superstition, it is unlucky for an engaged couple to hear their banns read in a church together.

A profusion of myrtle growing in a garden is an omen of a wedding in the household; however, a girl who is engaged to be married should never plant myrtle or it will cause her wedding to be called off, according to European superstition.

To give a spray of lilacs to one's betrothed is an omen that the engagement will soon be broken off.

To dream about eggs portends that you will soon be engaged to your true love.

If an engaged couple is photographed together before their wedding day, they will soon part.

If a girl turns down a proposal while at a dance, she will receive good luck in the near future.

To alter, break, or lose an engagement ring before the wedding ceremony is an omen that the engaged couple are not suited for each other.

If a betrothed girl drops a fork while setting the dinner table, it is a sign that her engagement will soon be broken.

Bridesmaids

A bridesmaid who stumbles while walking down the aisle is destined to become an "old maid" for the rest of her life.

To be a bridesmaid three times guarantees spinsterhood. However, it is said that being a bridesmaid seven times breaks the power of the jinx.

A bridesmaid who catches the bride's bouquet (or garter, as is the wedding custom in France) when it is thrown will be the next to marry.

A bride's old shoes are a powerful charm, and when worn by a bridesmaid, the chances of her getting married are greatly increased.

Good fortune is indicated if a bridesmaid throws away a pin on the wedding day. However, it is an omen of bad luck if she should be accidentally pricked by one.

Marriage

A butterfly in the house is an omen that there will soon be a wedding.

If you catch a dragonfly, you will fall in love and marry before the end of the year.

According to folk belief in Finland and Brittany, if an unmarried girl hears the call of a cuckoo, she will marry her true love before the coming winter.

To see three crows flying together portends a marriage in the near future.

If the first bird an unmarried girl sees on Saint Valentine's Day is a woodpecker, it is an omen that she will never wed.

A hummingbird picking at a young girl's food is an omen of marriage.

When two spoons are found together in the same saucer, it presages a wedding in the family.

According to an old European folk superstition, a vein on the bridge of a person's nose is a sign that he or she will never wed.

Young boys who put on their first pair of long pants on Good Friday will be assured of a happy marriage.

If two unmarried girls pull apart a wishbone, the girl who breaks off the bigger half will be the first of the two to marry.

Accidentally knocking out a candle is a lucky sign that there will be a wedding in the near future.

If a man lights his pipe from a lamp of any kind, he will have a troublesome or unfaithful wife, according to an old folk superstition in France.

A German folk superstition claims that when a girl falls asleep while she is working, or if she accidentally gets a thorn caught on her dress, it is an omen that she will marry a widower.

If a young girl sings at the table or constantly splashes

herself with water while washing her laundry, her future husband will be a drunkard, according to folk superstition in America as well as Britain.

According to an old German tradition based on superstition, sisters should never marry on the same day or within a year of each other or the marriages will be ill-fated.

If two sisters marry two brothers, one of the marriages will be unlucky. It is also unlucky to marry someone from your own family.

It is considered unlucky for a woman to marry a man whose name begins with the same letter as hers. It is even more unlucky to marry a person with the same last name, according to an old verse which country folk in England still repeat: "Change your name and not the letter, you change for worse and not for better."

A woman who accidentally breaks an earthen pot while thinking of her husband (or fiancé) will have a happy marriage for as many years as there are broken pieces.

It is unlucky to get married on your birthday; however, it is particularly lucky for a bride and groom to share the same birthday.

It is unlucky to get married on a Friday, and even unluckier if the Friday happens to fall on the thirteenth of May, according to the Romans.

Never marry when the moon is in a waning phase or three days after a new moon. For a long and happy marriage, the wedding should take place at the time of a new moon.

Good luck comes to those who get married on Saint Valentine's Day or on the last day of the year. It is also said that Wednesday is a lucky day for weddings. If you marry on a Tuesday, you will be blessed with riches.

It is an old saying that a woman who marries on April Fool's Day will be the one to "wear the pants" in the marriage.

It is unlucky to postpone a wedding date or to get mar-

ried on any of the following days: February 11, any day in
the month of May, any day in Lent, June 2, November 2
(All Soul's Day), December 1, or December 28 (Holy Inno-
cent's Day).

Rain on a wedding day will bring ill luck to the marriage.

It is extremely unlucky for a wedding to take place after
sunset. According to folk superstition, those who wed after
darkness falls will lose their children and die an early death.

To ensure a happy marriage, a kettle of boiling water
should be poured over the doorstep after the bride leaves
her parents' house.

In Japan it is considered unlucky to sweep a bride's
room after she has left for the wedding ceremony.

If a bride scatters bread crumbs while on her way to the
church, she will receive future happiness.

For good luck, a stitch should be added to a bride's wedding gown just before she leaves for the church.

It is bad luck for a wedding party to see a pig or a fu-
neral cortege while on the way to the church.

To see a toad or a robin while on the way to the church is
a good omen for a bride and groom, but if a dog should
pass between them, the marriage will be doomed.

To see a rainbow on your wedding day is an omen of
good luck and future happiness.

It is an omen of good luck for a bride's path to be crossed
by a chimney sweep, a black cat, or an elephant.

A man who forgets his hat on his wedding day will be
an unfaithful husband.

If a bride places in her pocket before the wedding ceremony a pierced coin or a penny bearing the date of her
birth, she will receive good fortune.

An open grave in the churchyard during the wedding
ceremony is a bad omen.

If a bride leaps over a robe or stool at the church gate,
she will lose her sense of humor.

The marriage will be ill-fated if the groom sees the bride on the wedding day before they meet at the church.

The marriage will be happy and blessed if the bridesmaids lay out the bride's stockings in the shape of a cross.

To avoid bad luck, a bride in her full bridal outfit should never look at her reflection in a mirror on her wedding day until after the ceremony.

It is lucky for a bride to wear orange blossoms or a pair of old shoes. If a bride wears the same pair of shoes that her mother wore at her wedding, she will be blessed with riches and good health.

To ensure a long and happy marriage, according to an ancient (and still popular) wedding tradition, a bride must wear to her wedding "something old, something new, something borrowed, and something blue."

You'll be a wealthy bride if you wear a stocking with a hole at the side.

A bride who tears her wedding gown or bursts a seam will be mistreated by her husband.

Blood on a wedding gown in an omen of an early death.

It is extremely unlucky for a bride to make her own wedding gown.

A bride who wears a silk wedding gown will have good luck, especially if the gown was worn by her mother or grandmother. A bride who wears satin will be cursed with misfortune, and a bride who wears a gown of velvet will die in poverty.

It is bad luck for a groom to wear black, purple, or green at his wedding.

If a bride weeps bitterly on her wedding day, a happy marriage is portended.

Light a white candle on your wedding day to ensure a long and happy marriage.

If a candle suddenly goes out by itself during a wedding ceremony, it is an omen that the marriage will end in sorrow.

Rice, which is an ancient symbol of fertility, brings good

luck and prosperity when thrown over a newlywed couple as they leave the church. (Before the custom of rice-throwing at weddings, it was traditional for an older married woman or the bride's mother to give the bride a bag of hazel nuts as she leaves the church to bestow her with fertility.)

Old shoes or boots tied to the back of a newlywed couples' car will bring good luck and a happy marriage.

It is an unlucky omen for a stone to roll across the path of a newly married couple.

It is unlucky for a bride to bake her own wedding cake or to taste her cake before the wedding day.

If a bride accidentally breaks a dish at her wedding banquet, it is a sign that her marriage will be an unhappy one, according to Scottish folk superstition.

A man must carry his new bride over the threshold, for it is bad luck for a bride to step over the doorstep when entering her new home.

If a bride falls asleep before her husband on the wedding night, it indicates that she will be the first to die.

If a cat sneezes or a hen cackles in the bride's home on the wedding eve, the marriage will be happy and blessed.

According to an old Scottish folk belief, it is an omen of bad luck for a clot of soot to fall down from the chimney during a newlywed couple's wedding breakfast.

If a wife loses her wedding ring, she will lose her husband's love, and vice versa. If her wedding ring breaks, it is an omen that both she and her husband will go to an early grave. To break the jinx, the husband should immediately place a new wedding ring on his wife's finger and repeat the lines of the marriage vow.

If a bride wears a coin in each of her shoes, she will have a happy marriage and wealth.

To see a shooting star on the night before your wedding is a good omen.

A man or woman who wears lilacs (except on May Day) will never marry.

Glossary of Terms

AIR: One of the four ancient and mystical elements.

AMULET: A consecrated object (usually a small, colored stone, or a piece of metal inscribed with runes or other magickal symbols) that possesses the power to draw love or good luck. Amulets are also used to protect against threatening influences, evil, and misfortune. Astrological jewelry, four-leaf clovers, and a rabbit's foot are several examples of popular modern amulets.

ATHAME: A ritual knife with a double-edged blade, used by Witches and magicians to draw circles and to store and direct energy during magickal rituals.

BELL: A hollow, metallic instrument, usually cup-shaped with a flared opening, which emits a tone when struck by a clapper suspended within or by a separate stick or hammer. Bells have been used by nearly all cultures throughout history as magickal talismans, fertility charms, summons to a deity, and as instruments for sacred music and religious rituals of widely varying beliefs. Many Witches use a consecrated bell as an altar tool to signal the beginning and/or close of a ritual or Sabbat.

BEWITCHMENT: The act of gaining power over another person by means of white or black magick; the act of casting a spell over another person.

BOLLINE: A white-handled knife used by Witches to harvest sacred herbs, cut wands, slice bread, and carve magickal symbols in candles and talismans.

BOOK OF SHADOWS: A secret diary of magickal spells and potion recipes kept by a Witch or a Coven.

BURIN: An engraving tool used by Witches and magicians to mark names or symbols ritually on athames, swords, bells, and other magickal tools.

CANDLE MAGICK: A form of sympathetic magick that uses colored candles to represent the people and things at which its spells are directed.

CAULDRON: A small, black cast iron pot used by Witches that symbolically combines the influences of the four ancient elements, represents the womb of the Goddess, and is used for various purposes, including brewing potions, burning incense, and holding charcoal or herbs.

CENSER: A fireproof incense burner used in magickal rituals, and symbolic of the element of Air.

CHALICE: A sacred cup or goblet used by Witches to hold consecrated water or wine, and to symbolize the ancient element of Water.

CHARM: A highly magickal object that works like an amulet or talisman; a magickal song or incantation which is often chanted over an amulet or talisman to consecrate it and charge it with magickal energy.

CONE OF POWER: The ritual act of visualizing energy in the form of a spiral light rising from the circle, and directing it toward a specific goal or task.

CONSECRATION: The act, process, or ceremony of making something sacred; the ritual use of water and salt to exorcise negative energies and/or evil influences from ritual tools, circles, etc.

COVEN: A group of Witches, traditionally thirteen in number, who gather together to work magick and perform ceremonies at Sabbats and Esbats.

COVENER: A man or woman who is a member of a coven.

COVENSTEAD: The place where a coven meets regularly.

COWAN: Among Witches, a person who is not a Witch.

THE CRAFT: Witchcraft, Wicca, the Old Religion, the practice of folk magick.

DIVINATION: The occult science, art, and practice of discovering the unknown and foretelling events of the future by interpreting omens or by various methods such as Tarot cards, dice, crystal balls, Ouija boards, astrology, etc.

EARTH: One of the four ancient and mystical elements.

ELEMENTALS: Spirit-creatures that personify the qualities of the four ancient elements. Salamanders are the elemental spirits of Fire; Undines are the elemental spirits of Water; Sylphs are the elemental spirits of Air; Gnomes are the elemental spirits of Earth.

ELEMENTAL SIGNS: The signs of Fire, Water, Air, and Earth. Fire is the symbol of energy, individuality, and identity; Water is the symbol of life, love, and spirit; Air is the symbol of the mind; Earth is the symbol of strength, fertility, and the emotions.

ENCHANTMENT: Magick; the act of bewitching or casting a spell.

ESBAT: A regular meeting of a coven that is held during the full moon at least thirteen times a year. At an esbat, the coveners exchange ideas, discuss problems, perform special rites, work magick and healing, and give thanks and/or request help from the Goddess.

FIRE: One of the four ancient and mystical elements.

GRIMOIRE: A magickal workbook containing various spells, formulas, rituals, and incantations; any collection of magickal spells and formulas.

HANDFASTING: A pagan betrothal ceremony in which the hands of the bride and groom are tied together with a consecrated knotted cord to signify that they have been joined together in matrimonial union. A handfasting may be performed as either a legally binding wedding or as a non-legally binding spiritual commitment rite.

HANDPARTING: A Pagan ceremony that dissolves the marriage partnership of a man and a woman who are non-legally married to each other.

HOODOO: A type of folk magick which combines European traditions with the Voodoo rituals brought to the New World by African slaves.

KARMA: The law of cause-and-effect that applies to all of our actions and their consequences in this life or in future incarnations.

LIBATION: Water or wine which is ritually poured on an altar, on the ground, or on a sacred fire as an offering to the Goddess, Horned God, or other deity.

LOVE POTION: An herbal aphrodisiac used in magickal spells with incantations to arouse love or sexual passion; a philtre.

MAGICK: The art, science, and practice of producing "supernatural" effects, causing change to occur in conformity, and controlling events in Nature with will.

MAGICK SQUARES: Powerful magickal talismans made from rows of numbers of letters of the alphabet arranged so that the words may read horizontally or vertically as palindromes, and the numbers total the same when added up in either direction.

MOJO BAG: a small leather or flannel bag filled with a variety of magickal items such as herbs, stones, feathers, bones, etc., and carried or worn as a charm to attract or dispel certain influences.

PENTACLE: A flat, round object bearing the motif of the mystical five-pointed pentagram star, and used in magickal ceremonies and spells to represent feminine energy and the ancient element of Earth.

PENTAGRAM: The symbol of the five-pointed star within a circle which represents the elements of Fire, Water, Air, and Earth, surmounted by the Spirit. The pentagram symbol is used by many Witches and magicians in various spells and magickal ceremonies.

PHILTRE: A love potion.

POPPET: A specially prepared herb-stuffed cloth doll that is used in sympathetic magick rituals to represent the person at whom the spell is directed.

POTION: An herbal tea or brew used in a magickal ritual.

RITUAL: A religious or magickal ceremony characterized by symbolic attire and formalized behavior, and designed to produce desired effects such as spiritual illumination or supernatural power, or to invoke a specific deity.

SABBAT: One of the eight Wiccan festivals; the gathering of Witches to celebrate at specific times of the year transitions in the seasons. The four major Sabbats are: Candlemas, Beltane, Lammas, and Samhain. The four minor ones are: Spring Equinox, Summer Solstice, Autumnal Equinox, and Winter Solstice (which is often called Yule).

SAINT AGNES' EVE: The night of January 20, when (according to folk legend) an unmarried woman will see her future husband or lover in a dream. Saint Agnes' Eve (named after the Roman Catholic child martyr who was beheaded in 304 A.D. for refusing to marry) was also the time when medieval Witches cast love spells and prepared love philtres and charms.

SAINT JOHN'S EVE: The night before Midsummer's Day. Saint John's Eve (June 23) is a traditional time for Witches to gather herbs for spells and love potions, for it is believed that the magickal properties of plants are greatest on this night.

SCEPTER: A wand used in magickal ceremonies and rituals.

SKYCLAD: Ritual nudity.

SMUDGING: The burning of incense or herbs to drive away negative forces and to purify the space in which magick is to be performed.

SOLITARY: A Witch who practices magick without belonging to a coven.

SPELL: An incantational formula; a nonreligious magickal ritual performed by a Witch, wizard, or magician.

SPELLCASTER: One who casts spells; a Witch.

THREEFOLD LAW: In Wicca, the belief that if one does good, he or she will get it back threefold in the same lifetime. Whatever harm one does to others is also returned threefold. (It is also known as Triple Karma.)

THURIBLE: A shallow, three-legged dish used in magickal workings, as an incense burner.

UNCTION: The act of anointing with an oil or an herbal ointment as part of a consecration, magickal ceremony, or healing ritual.

VISUALIZATION: In magick, the process of forming mental images of needed goals during rituals and spellcasting. (Also called Creative Visualization and Magickal Visualization.)

WAND: A wooden stick used to trace circles, draw magickal symbols on the ground, direct energy, and stir cauldron brews. The wand is the emblem of power. It represents the element of Air, and is sacred to the Pagan deities.

WATER: One of the four ancient and mystical elements.

WICCA: An alternative name for modern Witchcraft; a Neo-Pagan nature religion with spiritual roots in Shamanism, having one main tenet: the Wiccan Rede.

WICCAN REDE: A simple and benevolent moral code of Wiccans expressed as follows: "An it harm none, do what thou wilt."

WITCH: A man or woman who practices Witchcraft; a Wiccan; one who worships the gods of the Old Religion.

WITCHCRAFT: The Old Religion; the Craft of the Wise; the practice of folk religion that combines magick, nature worship, divination, and herbalism with bits and pieces of various pre-Christian religious beliefs, notably the Druids and the ancient Egyptians.

WITCHES' SABBAT: See *SABBAT.*

WIZARD: A male Witch or magician.

Bibliography

Ashley, Leonard. *The Amazing World of Superstition, Prophecy, Luck, Magic and Witchcraft*. New York: Bell, 1988.

Beyerl, Paul. *The Master Book of Herbalism*. Custer, Washington: Phoenix Publishers, 1984.

Bulfinch, Thomas. *The Age of Fable*. New York: Heritage Press, 1958.

Cunningham, Scott. *Encyclopedia of Magickal Herbs*. St. Paul, Minnesota: Llewellyn Publications.

Cunningham, Scott. *The Magickal Household*. St. Paul, Minnesota: Llewellyn Publications, 1987.

De Givry, Grillot. *Witchcraft, Magic and Alchemy,* tr. by J. Courtenay Locke. New York: Dover, 1971.

Dunwich, Gerina. *Candlelight Spells*. Secaucus, New Jersey: Citadel Press, 1988.

Dunwich, Gerina. *The Concise Lexicon of the Occult*. Secaucus, New Jersey: Citadel Press, 1990.

Dunwich, Gerina. *The Magick of Candle Burning*. Secaucus: New Jersey: Citadel Press, 1989.

Gibson, Walter B. and Litzka R. *The Complete Illustrated Book of the Psychic Sciences*. New York: Pocket Books, 1968.

Grieve, M. *A Modern Herbal*. New York: Dover Publications, 1971.

Hylton, William, H., editor. *The Rodale Herb Book*. Emmaus, Pennsylvania: Rodale Press, 1974.

Krochmal, Arnold and Connie. *A Guide to the Medicinal Plants*. New York: Quadrangle/New York Times Book Co., 1973.

Leach, Maria and Jerome Fried, editors. *Funk and Wagnall's Standard Dictionary of Folklore, Mythology and Legend*. New York: Harper and Row, 1984.

Lurker, Manfred. *Dictionary of Gods and Goddesses, Devils and Demons*. London: Routledge, 1988.

Lust, John. *The Herb Book*. New York: Bantam Books, 1974.

Murray, Alexander S. *Who's Who in Mythology*. New York: Crescent Books, 1988.

Sakoian, Frances and Louis S. Acker. *The Astrologer's Handbook*. New York: Harper and Row (Perennial Library Edition), 1989.

Valiente, Doreen. *An ABC of Witchcraft Past and Present*. Custer, Washington: Phoenix Publishing, 1988.

Walker, Barbara G. *The Women's Encyclopedia of Myths and Secrets*. New York: Harper and Row, 1983.

Waring, Philippa. *The Dictionary of Omens and Superstitions.* London: Souvenir Press, 1978.

Zolar. *Zolar's Encyclopedia of Ancient and Forbidden Knowledge.* Englewood Cliffs, New Jersey: Prentice-Hall, 1986.

Zolar. *Zolar's Encyclopedia of Omens, Signs and Superstitions.* Englewood Cliffs, New Jersey: Prentice-Hall, 1989.

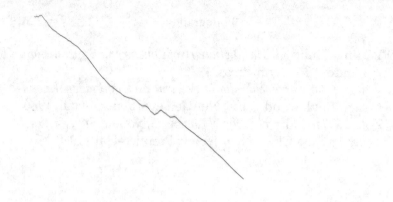

Index

Connect with Us

Visit us online at
KensingtonBooks.com
to read more from your favorite authors, see books
by series, view reading group guides, and more.

for sneak peeks, chances to win books and prize packs,
and to share your thoughts with other readers.

facebook.com/kensingtonpublishing
twitter.com/kensingtonbooks

Tell us what you think!

To share your thoughts, submit a review,
or sign up for our eNewsletters, please visit:
KensingtonBooks.com/TellUs.